The Child of the Islands

Caroline Norton

THE CHILD OF THE ISLANDS.

A Poem.

BY

THE
HON. MRS. NORTON.

"As half in shade, and half in sun,
  This world along its course advances,
May that side the Sun's upon
  Be all that shall ever meet thy glance!"

TO MY BROTHER,

RICHARD BRINSLEY SHERIDAN,

This Poem is dedicated

IN THE HOPE AND BELIEF THAT WE THINK ALIKE

ON ALL THE MORE IMPORTANT TOPICS TO WHICH IT
REFERS;

IN MEMORY OF MANY EARNEST CONVERSATIONS

HELD WITH HIM ON THOSE SUBJECTS;

AND IN TOKEN OF SYMPATHY WITH HIS UNWEARIED
EFFORTS

TO AMELIORATE THE CONDITION

AND PROMOTE THE HAPPINESS

OF ALL WHO ARE IN ANY WAY DEPENDENT UPON HIM.

"There is another topic which, I think, must force itself on your attention before long; I mean the condition of the people of England."

LORD JOHN RUSSELL, at the close of the Session of 1844.

"There is too little communication between classes in this country. We want, if not the feeling, at least the expression, of more sympathy on the part of the rich towards the poor; and more personal intercourse between them."

Speech of the HON. SIDNEY HERBERT, at the Salisbury Diocesan Church Meeting, Nov. 17, 1842.

"If the poor had more justice, they would need less charity."

JEREMY BENTHAM.

"Men who hate the whole theory of Political Economy with a hatred unspeakable, and consider it a most utter and iniquitous delusion, will yet reserve one clause. The one jewel in this Toad's head is the rule of not giving except for an exact equivalent."

Times Newspaper, Nov. 13, 1844.

"A high class, without duties to do, is like a tree planted on precipices, from the roots of which all the earth has been crumbling."

Past and Present, by THOMAS CARLYLE.

"Pallida mors æequo pulsat pede pauperum tabernas
Regumque turres."

HORACE, Ode iv.

"Æqua tellus
Pauperi recluditur
Regumque Pueris;" —

HORACE, Ode xviii.

PREFACE.

IT is, perhaps, scarcely necessary to inform my readers that the title of this Poem ("The Child of the Islands") has reference to His Royal Highness the Prince of Wales.

Had I been able to carry out my original plan, the volume now published would have appeared on the 9th of November, 1842, being the first anniversary of the birth of His Royal Highness. The recurrence of domestic affliction, in two consecutive autumns, compelled me to relinquish the literary tasks in which I was engaged; and I abandoned all thoughts of publishing at that particular time.

I hope and believe that this enforced delay has been favourable to the work, by enabling me to correct much that seemed crude and imperfect in the treatment of my subject. To the subject itself, the date is of little importance. The Child of the Islands was chosen, not as the theme of a Birthday Ode, or Address of Congratulation, but as the most complete existing type of a peculiar class—a class born into a world of very various destinies, with all the certainty human prospects can give, of enjoying the blessings of this life, without incurring any of its privations. I desired to contrast that brightness with the shadow that lies beyond and around. In the brief space of time since this poem was commenced, there has been great evidence of increasing attention to the sufferings, and to the endurance, of the lower classes. Much has been said—and something hass been done. Inquiries have been instituted; measures of relief have been passed; voice after voice, and spirit after spirit, among the noble-hearted and influential, have risen to support the cause of the helpless; till the reign of Victoria bids fair to claim a more hallowed glory than that which encircled the "Golden Age" of Elizabeth. The Feeble are calling (not vainly) on the Strong; the hoarse wail of the shipwrecked is answered by a cheer of promise from the shore; men's hearts have been roused, and are listening as to the sound of a rallying cry.

It is true that, had I intended merely to illustrate the Difference of Condition, I might have chosen from among those who have heaped up riches or climbed to power. I selected the Prince of Wales as my illustration, because the innocence of his age, the hopes that hallow his birth, and the hereditary loyalty which clings to the throne, concur in enabling men of all parties, and of every grade in society, to contemplate such a type, not only without envy or bitterness, but with one common feeling of earnest good-will. There are none, however sore their own battle with Adversity, who will refuse to join in applying to "The Child of the Islands" the wish so beautifully expressed by our Minstrel-poet, Moore:

> "As half in shade, and half in sun,
>   This world along its course advances,
> May that side the Sun's upon
>   Be all that shall ever meet thy glances!"

Nor will the presence of this good-will weaken the contrast or destroy the argument. It is, on the contrary, a gleam of that union and kindliness of feeling between the Higher and Lower Classes, which it is the main object of the writer of these pages (and of far better, wiser, and more powerful writers,) to inculcate; a gleam which may fade into darkness or brighten into sunshine, but which no one who attentively observes the present circumstances of this country, can believe will remain unaltered.

I shall only add, that I have endeavoured to profit by the criticisms and suggestions made on former occasions, and that I hope the indulgence so often extended to me as an author, will not be withheld from this poem. I can truly copy the plea of quaint John Bunyan with respect to its pages, and say,

> "It came from mine own heart,—so, to my head,
> And thence into my fingers tricklëd;
> Then, to my pen,"—

and if I have executed my task imperfectly, it has not been for lack of earnest feeling in the cause which I have attempted to advocate.

3 Chesterfield Street, May Fair, March 20, 1845

THE ARGUMENT.

OPENING.

THE WELCOME GIVEN, AND REJOICING OVER, THE BIRTH OF A CHILD—A DEGREE OF WELCOME FOR ALL, HOWEVER POOR OR UNFORTUNATE, ON THEIR FIRST ENTRANCE INTO LIFE—THE EXCEPTIONS UNNATURAL—INFANTICIDE A MADNESS—THE PECULIAR WELCOME OF "THE CHILD OF THE ISLANDS," WITH GLADNESS, THANKSGIVING, AND PRAYER—EVEN THE EARTH APPEARS TO WELCOME HIM.

SPRING.

THE DELIGHTS OF SPRING—ITS VALUE TO THOSE WHO SELDOM TASTE ITS PLEASURES—THE SEMPSTRESS—THE TRAPPER IN THE MINES—THE WEAVER AT HIS LOOM—THE LADY OP FASHION—HYDE PARK AT INTERVALS—THE SERPENTINE—SUICIDE—TYBURN GATE AND GALLOWS—THE SLEEP OF THE HOMELESS WANDERER IN THE LOUNGE OF IDLERS—"THE CHILD OF THE ISLANDS"—HIS SHARE OF WHAT SPRING CAN GIVE—THE INVENTIONS OF GENIUS— INVENTION THE SPRING OF INTELLECT—ARTIST-LIFE—THE DUTY OF ENCOURAGEMENT TO GENIUS IN OBSCURITY.

SUMMER.

ITS PLEASURES AND TOILS—THE WOODLANDS— MOONLIGHT BY LAND AND SEA—GIPSEY GIRL IN PRISON— THOUGHTS ON THE EDUCATION OF THE POOR—THE CHILD'S PRISON AT PARKHURST, IN THE ISLE OF WIGHT— THE IGNORANT THE WORST OFFENDERS—TRIAL OF A FELON—POWER OF LEADING THE MINDS OF OTHERS A TALENT ENTRUSTED TO US, FOR WHICH WE SHALL BE HELD ACCOUNTABLE—FATHER MATHEW—"THE CHILD OF THE ISLANDS"—HIS GUIDANCE AND EDUCATION A SUBJECT OF UNREMITTING CARE—THE CLAIM OF THE POOR AND IGNORANT ON HIS COMPASSION AND ASSISTANCE—THE OAKS OF WINDSOR—ENGLAND'S GLORY—THE SHIP— VICISSITUDES OF A SEA-LIFE.

AUTUMN.

ITS BEAUTY—THE MOORLANDS OF SCOTLAND—THE HEATHER BRAE—A SABBATH MORNING ON THE HILLS—CHURCH DISCORD—THE "FREE" CHURCH—SAINTS ON EARTH AND SAINTS IN HEAVEN—AN ENGLISH HARVEST—THE REAPER'S CHILD—HARVEST-HOME—PLENTY AND PRIVATION—VERDICT OF THE JURY: "STARVED TO DEATH"—THE CURSE SET ON THOSE WHO PERVERT THE JUDGMENT OF THE POOR—THE DEMAGOGUE—THE PATRIOT—THE NECESSITY AND DUTY OF EXERTION IN THE COMMON CAUSE—WHAT CAN I DO?—THE INDIVIDUAL VALUE OF EACH MAN'S HELP—THE WEAK AND STRONG ALIKE BOUND TO LABOUR—NEUTRALITY A SPECIES OF OPPRESSION—EVERY MAN HAS A LIFE—TASK ALLOTTED TO HIM.

WINTER.

THE SNOW ON THE GRAVES IN THE CHURCHYARDS OF ENGLAND—THE SNOW IN AFFGHANISTAN—THE SOLDIER'S GLORY—ARTHUR WELLESLEY—ARTHUR, DUKE OF WELLINGTON—DIFFERENT DESTINIES—THE WORN-OUT VETERAN—THE BLIND MAN'S WINTER—ALMS-GIVING—EXPENSIVE PLEASURES—THE BALLET-DANCER—CHRISTMAS CAROLS—CHRISTMAS PRIVATIONS—SICKNESS AMONG THE POOR—KINDNESS OF THE POOR TO EACH OTHER—CONTRAST OF THE SICK RICH MAN AND SICK POOR MAN—DECLINE OF LIFE—THE FEAR AND THE HOPE OF MEETING GOD—"THE CHILD OF THE ISLANDS"—HIS SHARE OF WHAT WINTER BRINGS.

CONCLUSION.

"THE CHILD OF THE ISLANDS" TRIED BY NONE OF THE ORDINARY GRIEVANCES OF THIS WORLD—DEATH OF THE DUKE OP ORLEANS; OF THE LATE DAUGHTER OF THE EMPEROR ALEXANDER; OF THE SON OF LEOPOLD OF BELGIUM; OF CIHARLOTTE OF ENGLAND AND HER SON—THE COMMON BROTHERHOOD OF MAN—DEATH OF TWO BABES IN OPPOSITE RANKS OF LIFE—THE EXISTENCE OF UNIVERSAL SYMPATHY A DECREE OF GOD—"THE CHILD OF THE ISLANDS"—THE MORAL OF GREATNESS BY DESCENT AND HERITAGE—THE END.

OPENING.

THE ARGUMENT.

The Welcome Given, and Rejoicing Over, the Birth of a Child—A Degree of Welcome for All, however Poor or Unfortunate, on their First Entrance into Life—The Exceptions Unnatural—Infanticide a Madness—The Peculiar Welcome of "The Child of the Islands," with Gladness, Thanksgiving, and Prayer—Even the Earth appears to Welcome Him.

I.

OF all the joys that brighten suffering earth,
    What joy is welcomed like a new-born child?
What life so wretched, but that, at its birth,
    Some heart rejoiced—some lip in gladness smiled?
    The poorest cottager, by love beguiled,
Greets his new burden with a kindly eye;
    He knows his son must toil as he hath toiled;
But cheerful Labour, standing patient by,
Laughs at the warning shade of meagre Poverty!

II.

The pettiest squire who holds his bounded sway
    In some far nook of England's fertile ground,
Keeps a high jubilee the happy day
    Which bids the bonfires blaze, the joybells sound,
    And the small tenantry come flocking round,
While the old steward triumphs to declare
    The mother's suffering hour with safety crowned;
And then, with reverent eyes, and grey locks bare,
Falters—"GOD bless the Boy!" his Master's Son and Heir!

III.

The youthful couple, whose sad marriage-vow
    Received no sanction from a haughty sire,
Feel, as they gaze upon their infant's brow,
    The angel, Hope, whose strong wings never tire—
    Once more their long discouraged hearts inspire;

Surely, they deem, the smiles of that young face,
    Shall thaw the frost of his relentless ire!
Homeward they turn in thought; old scenes retrace;
And, weeping, yearn to meet his reconciled embrace!

IV.

Yea, for this cause, even SHAME will step aside,
    And cease to bow the head and wring the heart;
For she that is a mother, but no bride,
    Out of her lethargy of woe will start,
    Pluck from her side that sorrow's barbéd dart,
And, now no longer faint and full of fears,
    Plan how she best protection may impart
To the lone course of those forsaken years
Which dawn in Love's warm light, though doomed to set in tears!

V.

The dread exception—when some frenzied mind,
    Crushed by the weight of unforeseen distress,
Grows to that feeble creature all unkind,
    And Nature's sweetest fount, through grief's excess,
    Is strangely turned to gall and bitterness;
When the deserted babe is left to lie,
    Far from the woeful mother's lost caress,
Under the broad cope of the solemn sky,
Or, by her shuddering hands, forlorn, condemned to die:

VI.

Monstrous, unnatural, and MAD, is deemed,
    However dark life's Future glooms in view,
An act no sane and settled heart had dreamed,
    Even in extremity of want to do!
    And surely WE should hold that verdict true,
Who, for men's lives—not children's—have thought fit
    (Though high those lives were valued at their due)
The savage thirst of murder to acquit,
By stamping cold revenge an error of crazed wit!([1])

VII.

> She—after pains unpitied, unrelieved—
>   Sate in her weakness, lonely and forlorn,
> Listening bewildered, while the wind that grieved,
>   Mocked the starved wailing of her newly born;
>   Racking her brain from weary night till morn
> For friendly names, and chance of present aid;
>   Till, as she felt how this world's crushing scorn,
> Passing the Tempter, rests on the Betrayed,—
> Hopeless, she flung to Death the life her sin had made!

VIII.

> Yes, deem her mad! for holy is the sway
>   Of that mysterious sense which bids us bend
> Toward the young souls new clothed in helpless clay,—
>   Fragile beginnings of a mighty end,—
>   Angels unwinged,—which human care must tend
> Till they can tread the world's rough path alone,
>   Serve for themselves, or in themselves offend.
> But God o'erlooketh all from His high throne,
> And sees, with eyes benign, their weakness—and our own!

IX.

> Therefore we pray for them, when sunset brings
>   Rest to the joyous heart and shining head;
> When flowers are closed, and birds fold up their wings,
>   And watchful mothers pass each cradle-bed
>   With hushed soft steps, and earnest eyes that shed
> Tears far more glad than smiling! Yea, all day
>   We bless them; while, by guileless pleasure led,
> Their voices echo in their gleesome play,
> And their whole careless souls are making holiday.

X.

> And if, by Heaven's inscrutable decree,
>   Death calls, and human skill be vain to save;
> If the bright child that clambered to our knee,
>   Be coldly buried in the silent grave;
>   Oh! with what wild lament we moan and rave!

What passionate tears fall down in ceaseless shower!
　There lies Perfection!—there, of all life gave—
The bud that would have proved the sweetest flower
That ever woke to bloom within an earthly bower!

XI.

For, in this hope our intellects abjure
　All reason—all experience—and forego
Belief in that which only is secure,
　Our natural chance and share of human woe.
　The father pitieth David's heart-struck blow,
But for himself, such augury defies:
　No future Absalom his love can know;
No pride, no passion, no rebellion lies
In the unsullied depth of those delightful eyes!

XII.

Their innocent faces open like a book,
　Full of sweet prophecies of coming good;
And we who pore thereon with loving look,
　Read what we most desire, not what we should;
　Even that which suits our own Ambition's mood.
The Scholar sees distinction promised there,—
　The Soldier, laurels in the field of blood,—
The Merchant, venturous skill and trading fair,—
None read of broken hope—of failure—of despair!

XIII.

Nor ever can a Parent's gaze behold
　Defect of Nature, as a Stranger doth;
For these (with judgment true, severe, and cold)
　Mark the ungainly step of heavy Sloth,—
　Coarseness of features,—tempers quickly wroth:
But those, with dazzled hearts such errors spy,
　(A halo of indulgence circling both:)
The plainest child a stranger passes by,
Shews lovely to the sight of some enamoured eye!

XIV.

The Mother looketh from her latticed pane—
    Her Children's voices echoing sweet and clear:
With merry leap and bound her side they gain,
    Offering their wild field-flow'rets: all are dear,
    Yet still she listens with an absent ear:
For, while the strong and lovely round her press,
    A halt uneven step sounds drawing near:
And all she leaves, that crippled child to bless,
Folding him to her heart, with cherishing caress.

XV.

Yea, where the Soul denies illumined grace,
    (The last, the worst, the fatallest defect;)
SHE, gazing earnest in that idiot face,
    Thinks she perceives a dawn of Intellect:
    And, year by year, continues to expect
What Time shall never bring, ere Life be flown:
    Still loving, hoping,—patient, though deject,—
Watching those eyes that answer not her own,—
Near him,—and yet how far! with him,—but still alone!

XVI.

Want of attraction this love cannot mar:
    Years of Rebellion cannot blot it out:
The Prodigal, returning from afar,
    Still finds a welcome, giv'n with song and shout!
    The Father's hand, without reproach or doubt,
Clasps his,—who caused them all such bitter fears:
    The Mother's arms encircle him about:(²)
That long dark course of alienated years,
Marked only by a burst of reconciling tears!

XVII.

CHILD OF THE ISLANDS! if the watch of love
    To even the meanest of these fates belong,
What shall THINE be, whose lot is far above
    All other fortunes woven in my song?
    To guard THY head from danger and from wrong,

5

What countless voices lift their prayers to Heaven!
Those, whose own loves crowd round, (a happy throng!)
Those, for whom Death the blessed tie hath riven;
And those to whose scathed age no verdant branch is given!

XVIII.

There's not a noble matron in the land,
    Whose christen'd heir in gorgeous robes is drest, —
There's not a cottage mother, whose fond hand
    Rocks the low cradle of her darling's rest, —
    By whom THOU art not thought upon and blest!
Blest for thyself, and for HER lineage high
    Who lull'd thee on her young maternal breast;
The Queenly Lady, with the clear blue eye,
Through whom thou claimest love, and sharest loyalty!

XIX.

They pray for THEE, fair child, in Gothic piles,
    Where the full organ's deep reverberate sound
Rolls echoing through the dim cathedral aisles,
    Bidding the heart with inward rapture bound,
    While the bent knee sinks trembling to the ground.
Till, at the signal of some well-known word,
    The white-robed choristers rise circling round;
Mingling clear voices with divine accord,
In Hallelujahs loud, that magnify the Lord!

XX.

They pray for THEE in many a village church,
    Deep in the shade of its sequester'd dell,
Where, scarcely heard beyond the lowly porch,
    More simple hymns of praise less loudly swell;
    Oft led by some fair form, — remember'd well
In after years among the grateful poor —
    Whose lot it is in lordly halls to dwell,
Thence issuing forth to seek the cotter's door,
Or tread with gentle feet the sanded schoolhouse floor.

XXI.

They pray for THEE, in floating barks that cleave
Their compass-guided path along the sea;
While through the topmast shrouds the keen winds grieve,
As through the branches of some giant tree;
And the surf sparkles in the vessel's lee.
Par from thine Albion's cliffs and native home,
Each crew of loyal mariners may be,
But, mingling with the dash of Ocean's foam,
That prayer shall rise, where'er their trackless course they roam.

XXII.

And where, all newly on some foreign soil
    Transplanted from the o'erpeopled Fatherland,
(Where hardy enterprise and honest toil
    Avail'd them not) the Emigrant's thin band,
    Gather'd for English worship, sadly stand;
Repressing wandering thoughts, which vainly crave
    The Sabbath clasp of some familiar hand,
Or yearn to pass the intervening wave
And wet with Memory's tears some daisy-tufted grave: —

XXIII.

There, even there, THY name is not forgot —
    Child of the land where they were children too!
Though sever'd ties and exile be their lot,
    And Fortune now with different aspect woo, —
    Still to their country and religion true,
From them the Indian learns, in broken phrase,
    To worship Heaven as his converters do;
Simply he joins their forms of prayer and praise,
And, in Thy native tongue, pleads for Thy valued days.

XXIV.

Yea, even Earth, the dumb and beautiful,
    Would seem to bid Thee welcome — in her way;
Since from her bosom thou shalt only cull,
    Choice flowers and fruits, from blossom and from spray.
    Spring — Summer — Autumn — Winter — day by day,

Above thy head in mystery shall brood;
And every phase of glory or decay,
And every shift of Nature's changeful mood,
To THEE shall only bring variety of good!

XXV.

No insufficient harvest's poverty,
One grain of plenty from thy store can take;
No burning drought that leaves green meadows dry,
And parches all the fertile land, shall make
The fountains fail, where thou thy thirst shalt slake!
The hardest winter that can ever bind
River, and running rill, and heaving lake,
With its depressing chain of ice, shall find
An atmosphere round THEE, warm as the summer wind!

XXVI.

From woes which deep privations must involve,
Set in luxurious comfort far aloof,
THOU shalt behold the vanishing snow dissolve,
From the high window and the shelter'd roof;
Or, while around thee, webs of richest woof
On gilded pillars hang in many a fold;
Read, in wise books, writ down for thy behoof,
(Sounding like fables in the days of old!)
What meaner men endure from want and pinching cold.

XXVII.

Oh, since this is, and must be, by a law
Of God's own holy making, shall there not
Fall on thy heart a deep, reflecting awe,
When thou shalt contemplate the adverse lot
Of those by men, but not by Heaven, forgot?
Bend to the lowly in their world of care;
Think, in thy Palace, of the labourer's cot;
And justify the still unequal share
By all they power to aid, and willingness to spare!

SPRING.

THE ARGUMENT.

The Delights of Spring—Its Value to those who seldom taste its
Pleasures—The Sempstress—The Trapper in the Mines—The
Weaver at his Loom—The Lady of Fashion—Hyde Park at
Intervals—The Serpentine—Suicide—Tyburn Gate and Tyburn
Gallows—The Sleep of the Homeless Wanderer in the Lounge of
Idlers—"The Child of the Islands"—His Share of what Spring can
Give—The Inventions of Man's Genius—Invention the Spring of
Human Intellect—Artist-Life—The Duty of Encouragement to
Genius in Obscurity.

I.

WHAT shalt THOU know of Spring? A verdant crown
    Of young boughs waving o'er thy blooming head:
White tufted Guelder-roses, showering down
    A fairy snow-path where thy footsteps tread:
    Fragrance and balm,—which purple violets shed:
Wild-birds,—sweet warbling in commingled song:
    Brooklets,—thin murmuring down their pebbly bed;
Or more abundant rivers,—swept along
With shoals of tiny fish, in many a silver throng!

II.

To THEE shall be unknown that weary pain,
    The feverish thirsting for a breath of air,—
Which chokes the heart of those who sigh in vain
    For respite, in their round of toil and care:
    Who never gaze on Nature fresh and fair,
Nor in sweet leisure wile an hour away;
    But, like caged creatures, sullenly despair,
As day monotonously follows day,
Till youth wears on to age, and strength to faint decay.

III.

A feeble girl sits working all alone!
    A ruined Farmer's orphan; pale and weak;
Her early home to wealthier strangers gone,
    No rural beauty lingers on her cheek;
    Her woe-worn looks a woeful heart bespeak;
Though in her dull, and rarely lifted eye,
    (Whose glances nothing hope, and nothing seek,)
Those who have time for pity, might descry
A thousand shattered gleams of merriment gone by!

IV.

Her window-sill some sickly plants adorn,
    (Poor links to memories sweet of Nature's green!)
There to the City's smoke-polluted morn
    The primrose lifts its leaves, with buds between,
    'Minished and faint, as though their life had been
Nipped by long pining and obscure regret;
    Torn from the sunny bank where erst were seen
Lovely and meek companions, thickly set,—
The cowslip, rich in scent, and humble violet!

V.

Too fanciful! the plant but pines, like her,
    For purer air; for sunbeams warm and kind;
Th' enlivening joy of nature's busy stir,
    The rural freedom, long since left behind!
    For the fresh woodlands,—for the summer wind,—
The open fields with perfumed clover spread;—
    The hazel copse,—whose branches intertwined
Made natural bow'rs and arches overhead,
With many a narrow path, where only two could tread.

VI.

Never, oh! never more, shall these afford
    Her stifled heart their innocent delight!
Never, oh! never more, the rich accord
    Of feathered songsters make her morning bright!
    Earning scant bread, that finds no appetite,

The sapless life she toils for, lingers on;
　　And when at length it sinks in dreary night,
A shallow, careless grave is dug,—where none
Come round to bless her rest, whose ceaseless tasks are done!

VII.

And now, the devious threads her simple skill
　　Wove in a quaint device and flowery line,
Adorn some happier maid, whose wayward will
　　Was struck with wishing for the fair design:
　　Some "curléd darling" of a lordly line,
Whose blooming cheek, through veils of texture rare,
　　Mantling with youth's warm blood is seen to shine;
While her light garments, draped with modest care,
Soft as a dove's white wings, float on the breezy air.

VIII.

Oh, there is need for permanent belief
　　In the All-Equal World of Joy to come!
Need for such solace to the restless grief
　　And heavy troubles of our earthly home!
　　Else might our wandering reason blindly roam,
And ask, with all a heathen's discontent,(³)
　　Why Joy's bright cup for some should sparkling foam,
While others, not less worthy, still lament,
And find the cup of tears the only portion sent!

IX.

But for the Christian's hope, how hard, how cold,
　　How bitterly unjust, our lot would seem!
How purposeless and sad, to young and old!
　　How like the struggles of a torturing dream,
　　When ghastly midnight bids us strive and scream!
All fades—all fleets—of which our hearts grow fond;
　　Pain presses on us to the last extreme,—
When lo! the dawn upriseth, clear beyond,
And, radiant from the East, forbids us to despond.

X.

And many a crippled child, and aged man,
    And withered crone, who once saw "better days,"
With just enough of intellect to scan
    This gracious truth; uncheered by human praise,
    Patient plods through the thorn-encumbered ways:
Oh, trust God counts the hours through which they sigh,
    While His green Spring eludes their suffering gaze,
And flowers along Earth's spangled bosom lie,
Whose barren bloom, for them, must unenjoyed pass by!

XI.

So lives the little Trapper(4) underground;
    No glittering sunshine streaks the oozy wall;
Not e'en a lamp's cold glimmer shineth round
    Where he must sit (through summer days and all,
    While in warm upper air the cuckoos call,)
For ever listening at the weary gate
    Where echoes of the unseen footsteps fall.
Early he comes, and lingers long and late,
With savage men, whose blows his misery aggravate.

XII.

Yet sometimes, (for the heart of childhood is
    A thing so pregnant with joy's blessed sun,
That all the dismal gloom that round him lies
    Can scarce suffice to bid its rays begone)
    In lieu of vain complaint, or peevish moan,
A feeble SONG the passing hour will mark!
    Poor little nightingale! that sing'st alone,
Thy cage is very low, and bitter dark;
But God hears thee, who hears the glad upsoaring lark.

XIII.

God seeth thee, who sees the prosperous proud
    Into the sunshine of their joy go forth:
God marks thee, weak one, in the human crowd,
    And judgeth all thy grief, (as all their mirth,)
    Bird with the broken wing that trails on earth!

12

His angels watch thee, if none watch beside,
   As faithfully—despite thy lowly birth—
As the child-royal of the queenly bride,
Or our belief is vain in Christ the Crucified!

XIV.

   In Christ! who made young children's guileless lives
     The cherished objects of His love and care;
Who bade each sinner that for pardon strives,
     Low, at Heaven's feet, a child-like heart lay bare;
     Opening the world's great universal prayer
With these meek words: "Our Father!" Strange, that we
     The common blessings of His earth and air
Deny to those who, circling round His knee,
Embraced, in mortal life, His immortality!

XV.

   Those "common blessings!" In this chequered scene
     How scant the gratitude we shew to God!
Is it, in truth, a privilege so mean
     To wander with free footsteps o'er the sod,
     See various blossoms paint the valley clod,
And all things into teeming beauty burst?
     A miracle as great as Aaron's rod,
But that our senses, into dulness nurst,
Recurring Custom still with Apathy hath curst.

XVI.

   They who have rarest joy, know Joy's true measure;
     They who most suffer, value Suffering's pause;
They who but seldom taste the simplest pleasure,
     Kneel oftenest to the Giver and the Cause.
     Heavy the curtains feasting Luxury draws,
To hide the sunset and the silver night;
     While humbler hearts, when Care no longer gnaws,
And some rare holiday permits delight,
Lingering, with love would watch that earth-enchanting sight.

XVII.

So sits the pallid weaver at his loom,
    Copying the wreaths the artist-pencil drew;
In the dull confines of his cheerless room
    Glisten those tints of rich and living hue.
    The air is sweet, the grass is fresh with dew,
And feverish aches are throbbing in his veins,
    But his are work-day Springs, and Summers too;
And if he quit his loom, he leaves his gains—
That gorgeous, glistering silk, designed with so much pains!

XVIII.

It shall be purchased as a robe of state
    By some great lady, when his toil is done;
While on her will obsequious shopmen wait,
    To shift its radiance in the flattering sun:
    And as she, listless, eyes its beauty, none
Her brow shall darken, or her smile shall shade,
    By a strange story—yet a common one—
Of tears that fell (but not on her brocade,)
And misery weakly borne while it was slowly made.

XIX.

For while that silk the weaver's time beguiled,
    His wife lay groaning on her narrow bed,
The suffering mother of a new-born child,
    Without a cradle for its weakly head,
    Or future certainty of coarsest bread;
Not, in that hour of Nature's sore affright,
    A fire, or meal that either might be fed;
So, through the pauses of the dreadful night,
Patient they lay, and longed for morning's blessed light.(5)

XX.

Not patient—no; I over-rate his strength
    Who listened to the infant's wailing cry,
And mother's weary moan, until at length
    He gave them echo with a broken sigh!
    Daylight was dawning, and the loom stood nigh:

14

He looked on it, as though he would discern
　　If there was light enough to labour by.
What made his heart's-blood leap, and sink, in turn?
What, in that cold gloom caused his pallid cheek to burn?

XXI.

What made him rise, with wild and sudden start?
　　Alas! the poor are weak, when they are tried!
(Can the rich say, that they, with steadfast heart,
　　Have all temptations constantly defied?)
　　He counts the value of that robe of pride;
And while the dawn clears up, that ushers in
　　His child's first morn on life's uncertain tide,
He keeps its birthday with a deed of sin,
And pawns his master's silk, bread for his wife to win.

XXII.

Let none excuse the deed, for it was wrong:—
　　And since 'twas ruin to the wretch employed,
No doubt the hour's despair was wild and strong
　　Which left that loom of silken splendours void:
　　Let Virtue trust their meal was unenjoyed,
Eaten in trembling, drenched with bitterness,—
　　And that the faint uncertain hope which buoyed
His heart awhile, to hide his guilt's excess,
And get that silk redeemed, was vain, from his distress:

XXIII.

So that true Justice might pursue her course;
　　And the silk, finished by "a different hand,"
Might in good time (delayed awhile perforce)
　　Be brought to clothe that lady of the land
　　Whom I behold as in a vision stand.
Lo! in my vision, on its folds are laid
　　The turquoise-circled fingers of her hand;
While by herself, and her attendant maid,
Its texture, soft and rich, is smiled on and surveyed.

XXIV.

Indifferent to her, the heavy cost
    Of that rich robe, first pawned for one poor meal;
She that now wears it, and her lord, may boast
    No payment made,—yet none dare say THEY steal!
    No, not if future reckoning-hours reveal
Debts the encumbered heir can never pay;
    But whose dishonest weight his heart shall feel
Through many a restless night and bitter day,
Hearing what cheated men of the bad dead will say.

XXV.

Onward she moves, in Fashion's magic glass,
    Half-strut, half-swim, she slowly saunters by:
A self-delighting, delicate, pampered mass
    Of flesh indulged in every luxury
    Folly can crave, or riches can supply:
Spangled with diamonds—head, and breast, and zone,
    Scorn lighting up her else most vacant eye,
Careless of all conditions but her own,
She sweeps that stuff along, to curtsey to the throne.

XXVI.

That dumb woof tells no story! Silent droops
    The gorgeous train, voluminously wide;
And while the lady's knee a moment stoops
    (Mocking her secret heart, which swells with pride,)
    No ragged shadow follows at her side
Into that royal presence, where her claim
    To be admitted, is to be allied
To wealth, and station, and a titled name,—
No warning voice is heard to supplicate or blame.

XXVII.

Nor,—since by giving working hands employ,
    Her very vanity must help their need
Whom, in her life of cold ungenerous joy,
    She never learned to pity or to heed,—
    Would sentence harsh from thoughtful minds proceed;

But that the poor man, dazzled, sees encroach
    False lights upon his pathway, which mislead
Those who the subject of his wrongs would broach,
Till Rank a bye-word seems,—and Riches a reproach.

XXVIII.

How oft some friendly voice shall vainly speak
    The sound true lessons of Life's holier school;—
How much of wholesome influence prove weak,
    Because one tinselled, gaudy, selfish fool,
    Hath made the exception seem the practiced rule!
In Luxury, so prodigal of show,—
    In Charity, so wary and so cool,—
That wealth appeared the poor man's open foe,
And all, of high estate, this language to avow:—

XXIX.

"A life of self-indulgence is for Us,
    "A life of self-denial is for them;
"For Us the streets, broad-built and populous,
    "For them, unhealthy corners, garrets dim,
    "And cellars where the water-rat may swim!
"For Us, green paths refreshed by frequent rain,
    "For them, dark alleys where the dust lies grim!
"Not doomed by Us to this appointed pain,—
"God made us, Rich and Poor—of what do these complain?"

XXX.

Of what? Oh! not of Heaven's great law of old,
    That brightest light must fall by deepest shade;
Not that they wander hungry, gaunt, and cold,
    While others in smooth splendours are arrayed;
    Not that from gardens where they would have strayed
You shut them out, as though a miser's gem
    Lay in the crystal stream or emerald glade,
Which they would filch from Nature's diadem;
But that you keep no thought, no memory of THEM.

XXXI.

>That, being gleaners in the world's large field
>   (And knowing well they never can be more,)
>Those unto whom the fertile earth must yield
>   Her increase, will not stand like him of yore,
>   Large-hearted Boaz, on his threshing-floor,
>Watching that weak ones starve not on their ground.
>   How many sills might frame a beggar's door,
>For any love, or help, or pity found,
>In rich men's hearts and homes, to help the needy round!

XXXII.

>Meanwhile, enjoy your Walks, your Parks, your Drives,
>   Heirs of Creation's fruits, this world's select!
>Bask in the sunshine of your idle lives,
>   And teach your poorer brother to expect
>   Nor share, nor help! Rouse up the fierce-toned sect
>To grudge him e'en the breeze that once a-week
>   Might make him feel less weary and deject;(6)
>And stand, untouched, to see how thankful-meek
>He walks that day, his child close nestling at his cheek.

XXXIII.

>Compel him to your creed; force him to think;
>   Cut down his Sabbath to a day of rest
>Such as the beasts enjoy, — to eat, and drink,
>   And drone away his time, by sleep opprest: —
>   But let "My lady" send, at her behest,
>A dozen different servants to prepare,
>   Grooms, coachmen, footmen, in her livery drest,
>And shining horses, fed with punctual care,
>To whirl her to Hyde Park, that she may "take the air."

XXXIV.

>Yet, even with her, we well might moralise;
>   (No place too gay, if so the heart incline!)
>For dark the Seal of Death and Judgment lies
>   Upon thy rippling waters, Serpentine!
>   Day after day, drawn up in linkèd line,

Your lounging beauties smile on idle men,
　　Where Suicides have braved the Will Divine,
　Watched the calm flood that lay beneath their ken,
Dashed into seeming peace, and never rose again!

XXXV.

There, on the pathway where the well-groomed steed
　　Restlessly paws the earth, alarmed and shy;
While his enamoured rider nought can heed
　　Save the soft glance of some love-lighted eye;
　　There, they dragged out the wretch who came to die
There was he laid—stiff, stark, and motionless,
　　And searched for written signs to notify
What pang had driv'n him to such sore excess,
And who should weep his loss, and pity his distress!

XXXVI.

Cross from that death-pond to the farther side,
　　Where fewer loiterers wander to and fro,
There,—buried under London's modern pride,
　　And ranges of white buildings,—long ago
　　Stood Tyburn Gate and gallows! Scenes of woe,
Bitter, heart-rending, have been acted here;
　　While, as he swung in stifling horrid throe,
Hoarse echoes smote the dying felon's ear,
Of yells from fellow-men, triumphant in his fear!

XXXVII.

Not always thus. At times a Mother knelt,
　　And blest the wretch who perished for his crime;
Or a young wife bowed down her head, and felt
　　Her little son an orphan from that time;
　　Or some poor frantic girl, whose love sublime
In the coarse highway robber could but see
　　Her heart's ideal, heard Death's sullen chime
Shivering and weeping on her fainting knee,
And mourned for him who hung high on the gallows-tree.

XXXVIII.

Nowhere more deeply stamped the trace of gloom
   Than in this light haunt of the herding town;
Marks of the world's Forgotten Ones, on whom
   The eye of God for ever looketh down,
   Still pitiful, above the human frown,
As Glory o'er the Dark! Earth's mercy tires!
   But Heaven hath stored a mercy of its own,
Watching the feet that tread among the briars,
And guiding fearful eyes, when fainter light expires.

XXXIX.

Yet no such serious thoughts their minds employ,
   Who lounge and wander 'neath the sunshine bright,
But how to turn their idleness to joy,
   Their weariness to pleasure and delight;
   How best with the ennui of life to fight
With operas, plays, assemblies, routs, and balls—
   The morning passed in planning for the night
Feastings and dancings in their lighted halls;
And still, as old ones fade, some newer pleasure calls.

XL.

Betwixt the deathly stream and Tyburn Gate
   Stand withered trees, whose sapless boughs have seen
Beauties whose memory now is out of date,
   And lovers, on whose graves the moss is green!
   While Spring, for ever fresh, with smile serene,
Woke up grey Time, and drest his scythe with flowers,
   And flashed sweet light the tender leaves between,
And bid the wild-bird carol in the bowers,
Year after year the same, with glad returning hours.

XLI.

Oh, those old trees! what see they when the beam
   Falls on blue waters from the bluer sky?
When young Hope whispers low, with smiles that seem
   Too joyous to be answered with a sigh?
   The scene is then of prosperous gaiety,

Thick-swarming crowds on summer pleasure bent,
    And equipages formed for luxury;
While rosy children, young and innocent,
Dance in the onward path, and frolic with content.

XLII.

But when the scattered leaves on those wan boughs
    Quiver beneath the night wind's rustling breath;
When jocund merriment, and whispered vows,
    And children's shouts, are hushed; and still as Death
    Lies all in heaven above and earth beneath;
When clear and distant shine the steadfast stars
    O'er lake and river, mountain, brake, and heath, —
And smile, unconscious of the woe that mars
The beauty of earth's face, deformed by Misery's scars;

XLIII.

What see the old trees THEN? Gaunt, pallid forms
    Come, creeping sadly to their hollow hearts,(7)
Seeking frail shelter from the winds and storms,
    In broken rest, disturbed by fitful starts;
    There, when the chill rain falls, or lightning darts,
Or balmy summer nights are stealing on,
    Houseless they slumber, close to wealthy marts
And gilded homes: — there, where the morning sun
That tide of wasteful joy and splendour looked upon!

XLIV.

There the man hides, whose "better days" are dropped
    Round his starvation, like a veil of shame;
Who, till the fluttering pulse of life hath stopped,
    Suffers in silence, and conceals his name: —
    There the lost victim, on whose tarnished fame
A double taint of Death and Sin must rest,
    Dreams of her village home and Parents' blame,
And in her sleep by pain and cold opprest,
Draws close her tattered shawl across her shivering breast.(8)

XLV.

Her history is written in her face;
    The bloom hath left her cheek, but not from age;
Youth, without innocence, or love, or grace,
    Blotted with tears, still lingers on that page!
    Smooth brow, soft hair, dark eyelash, seem to wage
With furrowed lines a contradiction strong;
    Till the wild witchcraft stories, which engage
Our childish thoughts, of magic change and wrong,
Seem realised in her—so old, and yet so young!

XLVI.

And many a wretch forlorn, and huddled group
    Of strangers met in brotherhood of woe,
Heads that beneath their burden weakly stoop,—
    Youth's tangled curls, and Age's locks of snow,—
    Rest on those wooden pillows, till the glow
Of morning o'er the brightening earth shall pass,
    And these depart, none asking where they go;
Lost in the World's confused and gathering mass,—
While a new slide fills up Life's magic-lantern glass.

XLVII.

CHILD OF THE ISLANDS! in thy royal bowers,
    Calm THOU shalt slumber, set apart from pain;
Thy spring-day spent in weaving pendent flowers,
    Or watching sun-bows glitter through the rain,
    Spanning with glorious arch the distant plain;
Or listening to the wood-bird's merry call;
    Or gathering sea-shells by the surging main;
And, wheresoe'er thy joyous glances fall,
The wise shall train thy mind, to glean delight from all.

XLVIII.

But most thou'lt love all young and tender things,
    And open wide and bright, in pleased surprise,
When the soft nestling spreads its half-fledged wings,
    Thy innocent and wonder-loving eyes,
    To see him thus attempt the sunny skies!(9)

Thou shalt enjoy the kitten's frolic mood,
  Pursue in vain gay-painted butterflies,
Watch the sleek puppy lap its milky food,
And fright the clucking hen, with all her restless brood.

XLIX.

Eager thou'lt gaze, where, down the river's tide,
  The proud swan glides, and guards its lonely nest;
Or where the white lambs spot the mountain's side,
  Where late the lingering sunshine loves to rest;
  Midst whom, in frock of blue and coloured vest,
Lies the young shepherd boy, who little heeds
  (The livelong day by drowsy dreams opprest)
The nibbling, bleating flock that round him feeds,
But to his faithful dog leaves all the care it needs.

L.

In time, less simple sights and sounds of Earth
  Shall yield thy mind a pleasure not less pure:
Mighty beginnings—schemes of glorious birth—
  In which th' Enthusiast deems he may secure,
  By rapid labour, Fame that shall endure;
Complex machines to lessen human toil,
  Fair artist-dreams, which Beauty's forms allure,
New methods planned to till the fertile soil,
And marble graven works, which time forbears to spoil.

LI.

For, like the Spring, Man's heart hath buds and leaves,
  Which, sunned upon, put forth immortal bloom;
Gifts, that from Heaven his nascent soul receives,
  Which, being heavenly, shall survive the tomb.
  In its blank silence, in its narrow gloom,
The clay may rest which wrapped his human birth;
  But, all unconquered by that bounded doom,
The Spirit of his Thought shall walk the earth,
In glory and in light, midst life, and joy, and mirth.

LII.

Thou'rt dead, oh, Sculptor—dead! but not the less
   (Wrapped in pale glory from th' illumined shrine)
Thy sweet St. Mary stands in her recess,
   Worshipped and wept to, as a thing divine:
   Thou'rt dead, oh, Poet!—dead, oh, brother mine!
But not the less the curbèd hearts stoop low
   Beneath the passion of thy fervent line:
And thou art dead, oh, Painter! but not so
Thy Inspiration's work, still fresh in living glow.

LIII.

These are the rulers of the earth! to them
   The better spirits due allegiance own;
Vain is the might of rank's proud diadem,
   The golden sceptre, or the jewelled crown;
   Beyond the shadow of a mortal frown
Lofty they soar! O'er these, pre-eminent,
   God only, Sovran regnant, looketh down,
God! who to their intense perception lent
All that is chiefest good and fairest excellent.

LIV.

Wilt thou take measure of such minds as these,
   Or sound, with plummet-line, the Artist-Heart?
Look where he meditates among the trees—
   His eyelids full of love, his lips apart
   With restless smiles; while keen his glances dart,
Above—around—below—as though to seek
   Some dear companion, whom, with eager start,
He will advance to welcome, and then speak
The burning thoughts for which all eloquence is weak.

LV.

How glad he looks! Whom goeth he to meet?
   Whom? God:—there is no solitude for him.
Lies the earth lonely round his wandering feet?
   The birds are singing in the branches dim,
   The water ripples to the fountains' brim,

The young lambs in the distant meadows bleat;
  And he himself beguiles fatigue of limb
With broken lines, and snatches various sweet,
Of ballads old, quaint hymns for Nature's beauty meet!

LVI.

Love is too earthly-sensual for his dream;
  He looks beyond it, with his spirit-eyes!
His passionate gaze is for the sunset-beam,
  And to that fainting glory, as it dies,
  Belongs the echo of his swelling sighs.
Pale wingèd Thoughts, the children of his Mind,
  Hover around him as he onward hies;
They murmur to him "Hope!" with every wind,
Though to their lovely Shapes our grosser sight is blind.

LVII.

But who shall tell, when want and pain have crost
  The clouded light of some forsaken day,
What germs of Beauty have been crushed and lost,
  What flashing thoughts have gleamed to fade away?(10)
  Oh! since rare flowers must yet take root in clay,
And perish if due culture be denied;
  Let it be held a Royal boast to say,
For lack of aid, no heaven-born genius died;
Nor dwindled withering down, in desert-sands of Pride!

LVIII.

The lily-wand is theirs! the Angel-gift!
  And, if the Earthly one with failing hand
Hold the high glory, do Thou gently lift,
  And give him room in better light to stand.
  For round THEE, like a garden, lies the land
His pilgrim feet must tread through choking dust;
  And Thou wert born to this world's high command,
And he was born to keep a Heavenly Trust;
And both account to ONE, the Merciful and Just.

LIX.

Youth is the spring-time of untarnished life!
   Spring, the green youth of the unfaded year!
We watch their promise, midst the changeful strife
   Of storms that threaten and of skies that clear,
   And wait, until the harvest-time appear.
CHILD OF THE ISLANDS, may those springs which shed
   Their blossoms round thee, give no cause for fear;
And may'st thou gently bend, and meekly tread,
Thy garlanded glad path, till summer light be fled!

SUMMER.

THE ARGUMENT.

The Pleasures and Toils of Summer—The Woodlands—Moonlight by Land and Sea—Gipsey Girl in Prison—Thoughts on the Education of the Poor—The Child's Prison at Parkhurst, in the Isle of Wight—The Ignorant the Worst Offenders—Trial of a Felon—Power of Leading the Minds of others a Talent entrusted to us, for which we shall be held accountable—Father Mathew—"The Child of the Islands"—His Guidance and Education a subject of unremitting Care—The Claim of the Poor and Ignorant on his Compassion and Assistance—The Oaks of Windsor—England's Glory—The Ship—Vicissitudes of a Sea-life.

I.

FOR Summer followeth with its store of joy;
　　That, too, can bring thee only new delight;
Its sultry hours can work thee no annoy,
　　Veiled from thy head shall be its glowing might.
　　Sweet fruits shall tempt thy thirsty appetite;
Thy languid limbs on cushioned down shall sink;
　　Or rest on fern-grown tufts, by streamlets bright,
Where the large-throated deer come down to drink,
And cluster gently round the cool refreshing brink.

II.

There, as the flakèd light, with changeful ray
　　(From where the unseen glory hotly glows)
Through the green branches maketh pleasant way,
　　And on the turf a chequered radiance throws,
　　Thou'lt lean, and watch those kingly-antlered brows—
The lustrous beauty of their glances shy,
　　As following still the pace their leader goes,
(Who seems afraid to halt—ashamed to fly,)
Rapid, yet stately too, the lovely herd troop by.

III.

This is the time of shadow and of flowers,
    When roads gleam white for many a winding mile;
When gentle breezes fan the lazy hours,
    And balmy rest o'erpays the time of toil;
    When purple hues and shifting beams beguile
The tedious sameness of the heath-grown moor;
    When the old grandsire sees with placid smile
The sunburnt children frolic round his door,
And trellised roses deck the cottage of the poor.

IV.

The time of pleasant evenings! when the moon
    Riseth companioned by a single star,
And rivals e'en the brilliant summer noon
    In the clear radiance which she pours afar;
    No stormy winds her hour of peace to mar,
Or stir the fleecy clouds which melt away
    Beneath the wheels of her illumined car;
While many a river trembles in her ray,
And silver gleam the sands round many an ocean bay!

V.

Oh, then the heart lies hushed, afraid to beat,
    In the deep absence of all other sound;
And home is sought with loth and lingering feet,
    As though that shining tract of fairy ground,
    Once left and lost, might never more be found!
And happy seems the life that gipsies lead,
    Who make their rest where mossy banks abound,
In nooks where unplucked wild-flowers shed their seed;
A canvass-spreading tent the only roof they need!

VI.

Wild Nomades of our civilised calm land!
    Whose Eastern origin is still betrayed
By the swart beauty of the slender hand, —
    Eyes flashing forth from over-arching shade, —
    And supple limbs, for active movement made;

How oft, beguiled by you, the maiden looks
    For love her fancy ne'er before pourtrayed,
  And, slighting village swains and shepherd-crooks,
Dreams of proud youths, dark spells, and wondrous magic books!

VII.

Lo! in the confines of a dungeon cell,
    (Sore weary of its silence and its gloom!)
  One of this race: who yet deserveth well
    The close imprisonment which is her doom:
    Lawless she was, ere infancy's first bloom
Left the round outline of her sunny cheek;
    Vagrant, and prowling Thief;—no chance, no room
  To bring that wild heart to obedience meek;
Therefore th' avenging law its punishment must wreak.

VIII.

She lies, crouched up upon her pallet bed,
    Her slight limbs starting in unquiet sleep;
  And oft she turns her feverish, restless head,
    Moans, frets, and murmurs, or begins to weep:
    Anon, a calmer hour of slumber deep
Sinks on her lids; some happier thought hath come;
    Some jubilee unknown she thinks to keep,
  With liberated steps, that wander home
Once more with gipsy tribes a gipsy life to roam.

IX.

But no, her pale lips quiver as they moan:
    What whisper they? A name, and nothing more:
But with such passionate tenderness of tone,
    As shews how much those lips that name adore.
    She dreams of one who shall her loss deplore
With the unbridled anguish of despair!
    Whose forest-wanderings by her side are o'er,
  But to whose heart one braid of her black hair
Were worth the world's best throne, and all its treasures rare.

X.

The shadow of his eyes is on her soul—
    His passionate eyes, that held her in such love!
Which love she answered, scorning all control
    Of reasoning thoughts, which tranquil bosoms move.
    No lengthened courtship it was his to prove,
(Gleaning capricious smiles by fits and starts)
    Nor feared her simple faith lest he should rove:
Rapid and subtle as the flame that darts
To meet its fellow flame, shot passion through their hearts.

XI.

And though no holy priest that union blessed,
    By gipsy laws and customs made his bride;
The love her looks avowed, in words confessed,
    She shared his tent, she wandered by his side,
    His glance her morning star, his will her guide.
Animal beauty and intelligence
    Were her sole gifts,—his heart they satisfied,—
Himself could claim no higher, better sense,
So loved her with a love, wild, passionate, intense!

XII.

And oft, where flowers lay spangled round about,
    And to the dying twilight incense shed,
They sat to watch heaven's glittering stars come out,
    Her cheek down-leaning on his cherished head—
    That head upon her heart's soft pillow laid
In fulness of content; and such deep spell
    Of loving silence, that the word first said
With startling sweetness on their senses fell,
Like silver coins dropped down a many-fathomed well.

XIII.

Look! her brows darken with a sudden frown—
    She dreams of Rescue by his angry aid—
She dreams he strikes the Law's vile minions down,
    And bears her swiftly to the wild-wood shade!
    There, where their bower of bliss at first was made,

Safe in his sheltering arms once more she sleeps:
   Ah, happy dream! She wakes; amazed, afraid,
Like a young panther from her couch she leaps,
Gazes bewildered round, then madly shrieks and weeps!

XIV.

For, far above her head, the prison-bars
   Mock her with narrow sections of that sky
She knew so wide, and blue, and full of stars,
   When gazing upward through the branches high
Of the free forest! Is she, then, to die?
Where is he—where—the strong-armed and the brave,
   Who in that vision answered her wild cry?
Where is he—where—the lover who should save
And snatch her from her fate—an ignominious grave?

XV.

Oh, pity her, all sinful though she be,
   While thus the transient dreams of freedom rise,
Contrasted with her waking destiny!
   Scorn is for devils; soft compassion lies
   In angel-hearts, and beams from angel-eyes.
Pity her! Never more, with wild embrace,
   Those flexile arms shall clasp him ere she dies;
Never the fierce sad beauty of her face
Be lit with gentler hope, or love's triumphant grace!

XVI.

Lonely she perishes; like some wild bird
   That strains its wing against opposing wires;
Her heart's tumultuous panting may be heard,
   While to the thought of rescue she aspires;
   Then, of its own deep strength, it faints and tires:
The frenzy of her mood begins to cease;
   Her varying pulse with fluttering stroke expires,
   And the sick weariness that is not peace
Creeps slowly through her blood, and promises release.

XVII.

    Alas, dark shadows, press not on her so!
      Stand off, and let her hear the linnet sing!
    Crumble, ye walls, that sunshine may come through
      Each crevice of your ruins! Rise, clear spring,
      Bubbling from hidden fountain-depths, and bring
    Water, the death-thirst of her pain to slake!
      Come from the forest, breeze with wandering wing!
    There, dwelt a heart would perish for her sake,—
Oh, save her! No! Death stands prepared his prey to take.

XVIII.

    But, because youth and health are very strong,
      And all her veins were full of freshest life,
    The deadly struggle must continue long
      Ere the free heart lie still, that was so rife
      With passion's mad excess. The gaoler's wife
    Bends, with revolted pity on her brow,
      To watch the working of that fearful strife,
    Till the last quivering spark is out. And now
All's dark, all's cold, all's lost, that loved and mourned below.

XIX.

    She could not live in prison—could not breathe
      The dull pollution of its stagnant air,—(11)
    She, that at dewy morn was wont to wreathe
      The wild-briar roses, singing, in her hair,—
      She died, heart-stifled, in that felon-lair!
    No penitence; no anchor that held fast
      To soothing meditation and meek prayer,
    But a wild struggle, even to the last—
In death-distorted woe her marble features cast!

XX.

    And none lament for her, save only him
      Who choking back proud thoughts and words irate,
    With tangled locks, and glances changed and dim,
      Bows low to one who keeps the prison-gate,
      Pleading to see her; asking of her fate;

Which, when he learns, with fierce and bitter cries
　　(Howling in savage grief for his young mate)
　He curseth all, and all alike defies;—
Despair and fury blent, forth flashing from worn eyes!

XXI.

　With vulgar terror struck, they deem him wild—
　　Fit only for the chains which madmen clank.
　But soon he weepeth, like a little child!
　　And many a day, by many a sunny bank,
　　Or forest-pond, close fringed with rushes dank,
　He wails, his clenched hands on his eyelids prest;
　　Or by lone hedges, where the grass grows rank,
　Stretched prone, as travellers deem, in idle rest,
Mourns for that murdered girl, the dove of his wild nest.

XXII.

　Little recks he, of Law and Law's constraint,
　　Reared in ill-governed sense of Liberty!
　At times he bows his head, heart-stricken, faint;
　　Anon—in strange delirious agony—
　　He dreams her yet in living jeopardy!
　His arm is raised,—his panting breast upheaves,—
　　Ah! what avails his youth's wild energy?
　What strength can lift the withering autumn leaves,
Light as they drifting lie on her for whom he grieves!

XXIII.

　Her SPRING had ripened into Summer fruit;
　　And, if that fruit was poison, whose the blame?
　Not hers, whose young defying lips are mute—
　　Though hers the agony, though hers the shame—
　　But theirs, the careless crowd, who went and came,
　And came and went again, and never thought
　　How best such wandering spirits to reclaim;
　How earnest minds the base have trained and taught,
As shaping tools vile forms have into beauty wrought.

XXIV.

The land that lies a blank and barren waste
    We drain, we till, we sow, with cheerful hope:
Plodding and patient, looking yet to taste
    Reward in harvest, willingly we cope
    With thorns that stay the plough on plain and slope,
And nipping frosts, and summer heats that broil.
    Till all is done that lies within the scope
Of man's invention, to improve that soil,
Earnest we yet speed on, unceasing in our toil.

XXV.

But for the SOUL that lieth unreclaimed,
    Choked with the growth of rankest weeds and tares,
No man puts forth his hand, and none are blamed;
    Though plenteous harvest might repay his cares,
Though he might "welcome angels, unawares."
    The earth he delves, and clears from every weed,
    But leaves the human heart to sinful snares;
The earth he sows with costly, precious seed,
But lets the human heart lie barren at its need.

XXVI.

Once I beheld (and, to my latest hour,
    That sight unfaded in my heart I hold)
A bright example of the mighty power
    One human mind, by earnest will controlled,
    Can wield o'er other minds—the base and bold,
Steeped in low vice, and warped in conscious wrong;
    Or weaker wanderers from the Shepherd's fold,
Who, sinning with averted faces, long
To turn again to God, with psalm and angel-song.

XXVII.

I saw one man,(12) armed simply with God's Word,
    Enter the souls of many fellow-men,
And pierce them sharply as a two-edged sword,
    While conscience echoed back his words again;
    Till, even as showers of fertilising rain

Sink through the bosom of the valley clod,
   So their hearts opened to the wholesome pain,
And hundreds knelt upon the flowery sod,
One good man's earnest prayer the link 'twixt them and God.

XXVIII.

   That amphitheatre of awe-struck heads
     Is still before me: there the Mother bows,
   And o'er her slumbering infant meekly sheds
     Unusual tears. There, knitting his dark brows,
     The penitent blasphemer utters vows
   Of holy import. There, the kindly man,
     Whose one weak vice went near to bid him lose
   All he most valued when his life began,
Abjures the evil course which erst he blindly ran.

XXIX.

   There, with pale eyelids heavily weighed down
     By a new sense of overcoming shame,
   A youthful Magdalen, whose arm is thrown
     Round a young sister who deserves no blame;
     (As though like innocence she now would claim,
   Absolved by a pure God!) And, near her, sighs
     The Father who refused to speak her name:
   Her penitence is written in her eyes—
Will he not, too, forgive, and bless her, ere she rise?

XXX.

   Renounce her not, grieved Father! Heaven shall make
     Room for her entrance with the undefiled.
   Upbraid her not, sad Mother! for the sake
     Of days when she was yet thy spotless child.
     Be gentle with her, oh, thou sister mild!
   And thou, good brother! though by shame opprest;
     For many a day, amid temptations wild,
   Madly indulged, and sinfully carest,
She yearned to weep and die upon thy honest breast.

XXXI.

Lost Innocence! — that sunrise of clear youth,
Whose lovely light no morning can restore;
When, robed in radiance of unsullied truth,
Her soul no garment of concealment wore,
But roamed its paradise of fancies o'er
In perfect purity of thought—is past!
But He who bid the guilty "sin no more"
A gleam of mercy round her feet shall cast,
And guide the pilgrim back to heaven's "strait Gate" at last.

XXXII.

By that poor lost one, kneel a happier group,
Children of sinners, christened free from sin;
Smiling, their curled and shining heads they stoop,
Awed, but yet fearless; confident to win
Blessings of God; while early they begin
(The Samuels of the Temple) thus to wait
HIS audible voice, whose Presence they are in,
And formally, from this auspicious date,
Themselves, and their young lives, to HIM to dedicate.

XXXIII.

While, mingling with those glad and careless brows,
And ruddy cheeks, embrowned with honest toil;
Kneels the pale artisan (who only knows
Of Luxury—how best its glittering spoil,
Midst whirring wheels, and dust, and heat, and oil,
For richer men's enjoyment to prepare);
And ill-fed labourers of a fertile soil,
Whose drunkenness was Lethe to their care, —
All met, for one good hope, one blessing, and one prayer!

XXXIV.

I will not cavil with the man who sneers
At priestly labours, as the work of hell;
I will not pause to contradict strange fears
Of where the influence ends, begun so well;
One only thought remained with me to dwell,

For ever with remembrance of that scene,
    When I beheld hearts beat and bosoms swell,
And that melodious voice and eye serene
Govern the kneeling crowd, as he their God had been.

XXXV.

I thought, in my own secret soul, if thus,
    (By the strong sympathy that knits mankind)
A power untried exists in each of us,
    By which a fellow-creature's wavering mind
    To good or evil deeds may be inclined;
Shall not an awful questioning be made,
    (And we, perchance, no fitting answer find!)
"Whom hast THOU sought to rescue, or persuade?
Whom roused from sinful sloth? whom comforted, afraid?"

XXXVI.

For whom employed, —e'en from thy useless birth, —
    The buried Talent at thy Lord's command?
Unprofitable servant of the earth!
    Though here men fawned on thee, and licked thy hand
    For golden wealth, and power, and tracts of land;
When the Eternal Balance justly weighs,
    Above thee, in the ranks of heaven, shall stand,
Some wretch obscure, who through unnoticed days,
Taught a poor village school to sing their Maker's praise.

XXXVII.

A mournful memory in my bosom stirs!
    A recollection of the lovely isle
Where, in the purple shadow of thy firs
    Parkhurst!(13) and gloomy in the summer smile,
    Stands the CHILD'S PRISON: (since we must defile
So blest a refuge, with so curst a name)
    The home of those whose former home was vile;
Who, dogged, sullen, scoffing, hither came,
Tender in growth and years, but long confirmed in shame.

XXVIII.

Alas! what inmates may inhabit there?
    Those to whose infant days a parent's roof,
In lieu of a protection, was a snare;
    Those from whose minds instruction held aloof,
    No hope, no effort made in their behoof;
Whose lips familiar were with blasphemy,
    And words obscene that mocked at all reproof,
But never uttered prayer to the Most High,
Or learned one gentle hymn, His name to glorify.

XXXIX.

Th' Untaught, Uncared-for, 'neath whose stolid look
    The Scriptures might have lain, a block of wood,
Hewn to the shape and semblance of a book,
    For any thing they knew in it of good,
    Or any text they heard or understood.
THESE are your Prisoned Children! Germs of Men,
    Vicious, and false, and violent of mood,
Such as strange carelessness first rears, and then
Would crush the sting out by a death of pain!

XL.

But skilful hands have drawn the arrow's barb
    From the unfestered wound which Time shall heal!
And though 'tis mournful, in their prison garb,
    To see them trooping to their silent meal;
    And though, among them, many brows reveal
Sorrow too bitter for such childish hearts;
    Yet the most pitiful (if just) must feel
(E'en while the tear of forced compassion starts)
That blessed is the hope their suffering imparts!

XLI.

The Saved are there, who would have been the Lost;
    The Checked in crime, who might have been the Doomed;
The wildbriar buds, whose tangled path was crost
    By nightshade poison trailing where they bloomed!
    The Wrecked, round whom the threatening surges boomed,

Borne in this Life-boat far from peril's stress;
   The Sheltered, o'er whose heads the thunder loomed;
  Convicts (convicted of much helplessness;)
Exiles, whom Mercy guides through guilt's dark wilderness.

XLII.

I saw One sitting in that Island Prison
   Whose day in solitude was going down,
E'en as in solitude its light had risen!(14)
    His little savage sullen face, bent down,
    From all kind words, with an averted frown—
A world of dumb defiance in his scowl!
    Or, looking up, with gaze that seemed to own,
  "I scorn the smiting of your forced control;
My body scourge or slay, you shall not bend my soul!"

XLIII.

But one was weeping—weeping bitter tears!
   Of softer mould his erring heart was made;
And, when the sound of coming steps he hears
    Advancing to his lone cell's cheerless shade,
    He turns, half welcoming and half afraid,
 Trustful of pity, willing to be saved;
    Stepping half way to meet the proffered aid;
  Thankful for blessings kind and counsel grave;
Strange to this new sad life, but patient, calm, and brave.

XLIV.

Brave! for what courage must it not require
   In a child's heart, to bear those dreadful hours?
Think how WE find the weary spirit tire,
    How the soul sinks with faint and flagging powers,
    Pent in, in these indulgent lives of ours,
By one monotonous day of winter's rain!
    Woe for the prisoned boy, who sadly cowers,
  In his blank cell, for days of dreary pain,
Pining for human looks and human tones in vain.

XLV.

Nor let it be forgot, for these young spirits,
    (Although by gross and vulgar sin defiled,)
How differently judged were their demerits,
    Were each a noble's or a gentle's child.
    Are there no sons at college, "sadly wild?"
No children, wayward, difficult to rear?
    Are THEY cast off by Love? No, gleaming mild
Through the salt drops of many a bitter tear,
The rainbow of your hope shines out of all your fear!

XLVI.

For they are YOUNG, you say; and this green stem
    With shoots of good shall soon be grafted in:
Meanwhile, how much is FROLIC, done by them,
    Which, in the poor, is punishable SIN?
    Nor mark I this, a useless sigh to win,
(They lose their ground, who falsely, lightly chide,)
    But to note down how much your faith you pin
Upon the worth of that, to them supplied—
Revealed Religion's light, and Education's guide.

XLVII.

Yea, for yourselves and sons, ye trusted it,
    And knew no reed it was you leaned upon;
Therefore, whoso denies that benefit
    To meaner men in ignorance chained down,
    From each this true reproach hath justly won:—
"Oh, selfish heart! that owned the healing sure,
    Yet would not help to save MY erring son!"
They cry to you, "PREVENT!"—You cannot cure,
The ills that, once incurred, these little ones endure!

XLVIII.

The criminal is in the felon's dock:
    Fearful and stupified behold him stand!
While to his trial cold spectators flock,
    And lawyers grave, and judges of the land.
    At first he grasps the rail with nervous hand,

40

Hearing the case which learnedly they state,
 With what attention ignorance can command:
Then, weary of such arguing of his fate,
Torpid and dull he sinks, throughout the long debate.

XLIX.

Vapid, incomprehensible to him
 The skilful pleader's cross-examining wit;
His sullen ear receives, confused and dim,
 The shouts of laughter at some brilliant hit,
 When a shrewd witness leaves the Biter bit.
He shrinks not while the facts that must prevail
 Against his life, unconscious friends admit;
Though Death is trembling in the adverse scale,
He recks no more than if he heard the autumn gale.

L.

Oh, Eloquence, a moving thing art thou!
 Tradition tells us many a mournful story
Of scaffold-sentenced men, with noble brow,
 Condemned to die in youth, or weak and hoary,
 Whose words survived in long-remembered glory!
But eloquence of words the power hath not
 (Nor even their fate, who perished gaunt and gory)
To move my spirit like his abject lot,
Who stands there, like a dog, new-sentenced to be shot!

LI.

Look, now! Attention wakes, with sudden start,
 The brutish mind which late so dull hath been!
Quick grows the heavy beating at his heart!
 The solemn pause which rests the busy scene,
 He knows, though ignorant, what that must mean—
The Verdict! With the Jury rests his chance!
 And his lack-lustre eye grows strangely keen,
Watching with wistful, pleading, dreadful glance,
Their consultation cease, their foreman slow advance.

41

D

LII.

His home, his hopes, his life, are in that word!
    His ties! (for think ye not that he hath ties?)
Alas! Affection makes its pleading heard
    Long after better sense of duty dies,
    Midst all that Vice can do to brutalise.
Hark to the verdict—"Guilty!"—All are foes!
    Oh, what a sight for good, compassionate eyes,
That haggard man; as, stupified with woes,
Forth from the felon's dock, a wretch condemned he goes!

LIII.

A wretch condemned, but not at heart subdued.
    Rebellious, reckless, are the thoughts which come
Intruding on his sentenced solitude:—
    Savage defiance! gnawing thoughts of home!
    Plots to escape even now his threatened doom!
Sense of desertion, persecution!—all
    Choke up the fount of grief, and bid the foam
Stand on his gnashing lips when tears should fall,
And mock the exhorting tones which for repentance call!

LIV.

For if one half the pity and the pains,
    The charity, and visiting, and talk,
Had been bestowed upon that wretch in chains,
    While he had yet a better path to walk,
    Life's flower might still have bloomed upon its stalk!
He might not now stand there, condemned for crime,(15)
    (Helpless the horror of his fate to balk!)
Nor heard the sullen bell, with funeral chime,
Summon him harshly forth, to die before his time!

LV.

CHILD OF THE ISLANDS! thou, whose cradle-bed
    Was hallowed still with night and morning prayer!
Thou, whose first thoughts were reverently led
    To heaven, and taught betimes to anchor there!
    Thou, who wert reared with fond peculiar care,

In happiest leisure, and in holiest light!
    Wilt THOU not feed the lamp whose lustre rare
Can break the darkness of this fearful night,
Midst dim bewild'ring paths to guide faint steps aright?

LVI.

Wilt thou not help to educate the poor?
    They will learn something, whether taught or no;
The Mind's low dwelling hath an open door,
    Whence, wandering still uneasy, to and fro,
    It gathers that it should, or should not, know.
Oh, train the fluttering of that restless wing!
    Guide the intelligence that worketh woe!
So shall the Summer answer to the Spring,
And a well-guided youth an age of duty bring.

LVII.

Thus,—freed from the oppressive pang which chokes
    A young warm heart that pities men in vain,—
Thou'lt roam beneath thy Windsor's spreading oaks,
    And see Life's course before thee, clear and plain,
    And how to spare, and how to conquer, pain:
Or, greeting fair Etona's merry groups,
    Thou'lt think, not only for this noble train,
The dovelike wing of Science brooding stoops,
But shadows many a head that else obscurely droops!

LVIII.

Glad shalt thou roam beneath those oaks, fair Boy!
    While round thy conscious feet the earth's cold dust
Reflects a sunshine from the Poor Man's joy!
    There dream of England's Glory: nor distrust
    Thy cheering hopes, for men who seek to thrust
Cold counsel on thy young, inspired heart;
    Pleading that, though 'tis politic and just
To fill each studded port and loaded mart,
Utopian are the schemes free knowledge to impart!

LIX.

Yet shalt thou dream of England's commerce, too;
  And the tall spreading trees, — which, branching round,
Thy footsteps to their covert coolness woo, —
  Cast visionary shadows on the ground
  Of floating ships for distant stations bound.
Unheard shall be the wild-bird's song! Instead,
  Hoarsely the roar of fancied waves shall sound;
And o'er the shining sands thy soul shall tread,
With Albion's snowy cliffs high beetling o'er thy head!

LX.

Or Thought, in her strange chaos, shall display
  That proudest sight reserved for English eyes —
The building ship — which soon shall cleave its way
  Through the blue waters, 'neath the open skies.
  The stately oak is felled, and low it lies,
Denuded of its lovely branches — bare
  Of e'en the bark that wrapped its giant size
Roughly defying all the storms of air,
One fragment of its gnarled and knotted strength to tear.

LXI.

Out of its swelling girth are aptly hewn
  The timbers fitted for the massive frame;
By perfect rule and measurement foreshewn,
  Plank after plank, each answering to the same,
  The work goes on — a thing without a name —
Huge as a house, and heavy as a rock,
  Enough the boldest looker-on to tame,
Standing up-gazing at that monstrous block,
Whose grand proportions seem his narrow sense to mock.

LXII.

And ceaseless, hammering, shouting, pigmy forms
  Work, crawl, and clatter on her bulging sides:
Are those the beings, who, in Heaven's wild storms,
  Shall move that mass against opposing tides?
  One, tread her decks, with proud impetuous strides?

44

Others, through yawning port-holes point the gun,—
    Scattering the foe her glorious strength derides,
And shouting "Victory" for a sea-fight won?
Oh, magic rule of MIND, by which such works are done!

LXIII.

But, first, the Launch must send our ship afloat:
    Assembled thousands wait the glorious sight:
Gay-coloured streamers deck each tiny boat,
    And glistening oars reflect a restless light:
    Till some fair form, with smiles and blushes bright,(16)
And active hand (though delicate it seem)
    Advances to perform the "Christening Rite;"
The fragile crystal breaks, with shivering gleam,
And the grand mass comes forth, swift gliding, like a dream.

LXIV.

Now give her MASTS and SAILS!—those spreading wings
    Whose power shall save from many a dangerous coast!
Her ROPES, with all their bolts, and blocks, and rings;
    Her glorious FLAG, no foe shall dare to brave
    Who sees it come careering o'er the wave!
Give her, the HEARTS of OAK, who, marshalled all,
    Within her creaking ribs when tempests rave
And the fierce billows beat that echoing walls
Fearless and calm obey the Boatswain's mustering call.

LXV.

Give her, those giant ANCHORS, whose deep plunge
    Into the startled bosom of the Sea,
Shall give the eager sailor leave to lounge
    In port awhile, with reckless liberty.
    Soon shall his changeful heart impatiently,
For their unmooring and upheaving long;
    For "Sailing-orders" which shall set him free;
While his old messmates, linked in brawny throng,
Coil up the Cable's length—huge, intricate, and strong!)

LXVI.

Give her, her CAPTAIN! who, from that day forth,
    With her loved beauty all his speech shall fill;
And all her wanderings, East, West, South, and North,
    Narrate, — with various chance of good and ill, —
    As though she lived, and acted of free will.
Yet, let no lip with mocking smile be curled ; —
    These are the souls, that man with dauntless skill,
Our Wooden Walls; whose Meteor-flag, unfurled,
Bids England "hold her own" against th' united world!

LXVII.

Dear Island-Home! — and is the boast so strange
    Which bids thee claim the Empire of the Sea?
O'er the blue waters as we fearless range,
    Seem not the waves familiar friends to be?
    We knew them in the Country of the Free!
And now they follow us with playful race,
    Back rolling to that land of liberty,
And dashing round her rocks with rough embrace,
Like an old shaggy dog that licks its Master's face.

LXVIII.

Yea, and a Watch-dog too, if there be need!
    A low determined growl, when danger lowers,
Shall, from the gloomy port-holes, grimly speed,
    To rouse our Heroes, and our armed Powers.(17)
    Let the land-circled nations keep their towers,
Their well-scanned passports, and their guards secure, —
    We'll trust this floating, changeful wall of ours,
And, long as ocean-waves and rocks endure,
So long, dear Island-Home, we'll hold thy freedom sure!

LXIX.

Back to our ship! She breasts the surging tide;
    The fair breeze freshens in the flowing sheet!
With deafening cheers the landsmen see her glide,
    And hearts, that watch her progress, wildly beat.
    Oh! where and when shall all the many meet,

46

Who part to-day? That secret none may sound!
 But slowly falls the tread of homeward feet;
 And, in the evening, with a sigh goes round,
That brief, but thrilling toast, "Health to the Outward-Bound!"

LXX.

Health to the Outward-Bound! How many go
 Whose homeward voyage never shall be made!
Who but that drear Sea-Burial shall know,
 Which bids the corse the shifting flood invade!
 No grave—no stone beneath the cypress-shade,
Where mourning friends may gather round and weep,
 Whose distant wretchedness is yet delayed:
Orphans at home a jubilee may keep,
While Messmates' hands commit a Father to the deep!

LXXI.

Some, whom the cry of "FIRE!" doth overtake
 On the wide desert of the lonely seas,
Their vague escape in open boats shall make;
 To suffer quenchless thirst, and parched disease,
 And hunger-pangs the DEATH-LOT shall appease.(18)
Some, crashing wrecked in one stupendous shock,
 Endure more helpless rapid fate than these,
And vainly clinging to the foam-washed block,
Die, drifted like weak weeds from off the slippery rock.

LXXII.

Some, scarcely parted twice a cable's length
 From those who on the firm earth safely stand,
Shall madly watch the strained united strength
 And cheers and wavings of the gallant band,
 Who launch their life-boat with determined hand.
Ah! none shall live, that zealous aid to thank;
 The wild surge whirls the life-boat back to land,—
The hazy distance suddenly grows blank,—
In that last labouring plunge the fated vessel sank!

LXXIII.

And some shall plough their homeward track in vain,
    Dying, it may be, within sight of shore:
While others, (dreariest horror of the main!)
    Are vaguely "lost" and never heard of more.
    Ah, me! how many now such fate deplore,
As his(19) for whom Grief's wild and piercing cry
    Followed, e'er yet lamenting tears were o'er,
Shed for his brother; doomed, like him, to die
In youth,—but not like him without one kinsman nigh!

LXXIV.

Peace to thy woeful heart, thou grey-haired sire;
    Each, had he lived, his duty would have done:
Towards gallant deeds unwearied to aspire,
    Was thine own heritage to either son.
    Yet thou hast wept,—like him whose race is run,—(20)
Who rose a happy Father when the day
    Through morning clouds, with misty radiance shone;
But when at eve his ship got under way,
Left his unburied son in wild Algoa Bay!

LXXV.

His generous son, who risked his own young life
    Hoping another from that doom to save;
And battled nobly with the water's strife,
    E'er the green billows were his floating grave.
    Nor died alone, beneath the whelming wave;
Others,—less known perhaps,—not cherished less
    By those who for their presence vainly crave,—
Sank struggling down in utter weariness,
Lost in that wild dark night of terrible distress.

LXXVI.

Oh, hearts have perished, neither faint nor few,
    Whose names have left no echo save at home;
With many a gallant ship, whose fearless crew
    Set sail with cheerful hope their course to roam!
    Buried 'neath many a fathom's shifting foam,—

By the rude rocks of many a distant shore, —
    Their visionary smiles at midnight come
To those whose waking eyes their loss deplore, —
Dreaming of their return, who shall return no more!

LXXVII.

CHILD OF THE ISLANDS! some such saddening tales,
    Thou, in thine infancy, perchance shalt hear;
Linked with the names a Nation still bewails,
    And warrior-deeds to England's glory dear.
    Ah! let them not fall lightly on thine ear!
Though Death calmed down that anguish, long ago,
    The record is not ended; year by year
Recurring instances of loss and woe
Shall bid thee, for like grief, a like compassion show!

LXXVIII.

Neglect not, Thou, the sons of men who bled
    To do good service in the former time;
Slight not some veteran father of the Dead,
    Whose noble boys have perished in their prime.
    Accept not selfishly, the love sublime
And loyalty which in such souls hath burned.
    What though it be thy right; the lack, a crime?
Yet should no honest heart by thine be spurned —
True service paid with smiles, and thanks, is cheaply earned.

LXXIX.

Keep Thou the reverence of a youthful heart
    To Age and Merit in thy native land;
Nor deem CONDITION sets thee far apart:
    ABOVE, but not ALOOF, a Prince should stand:
    Still near enough, to stretch the friendly hand
To those whose names had never reached the throne,
    But for great deeds, performed in small command:
Since thus the gallant wearers first were known,
Hallow those names; although not Royal like thine own.

LXXX.

And let thy Smile be like the Summer Sun,
　　Whose radiance is not kept for garden-flowers,
But sends its genial beams to rest upon
　　The meanest blushing bud in way-side bowers.
　　Earth's Principalities, and Thrones, and Powers,
If Heaven's true Delegates on Earth they be,
　　Should copy Heaven; which giveth fertile Showers,
The Dew, the Warmth, the Balm, the Breezes free,
Not to one Class alone,—but all Humanity!

END OF SUMMER.

AUTUMN.

THE ARGUMENT.

The Beauty of Autumn—The Moorlands of Scotland—The Heather Brae—A Sabbath Morning on the Hills—Church Discord—The "Free" Church—Saints on Earth and Saints in Heaven—An English Harvest—The Reaper's Child—Harvest-Home—Plenty and Privation—Verdict of the Jury: "Starved to Death"—The Curse set on those who Pervert the Judgment of the Poor—The Demagogue—The Patriot—The Necessity and Duty of Exertion in the Common Cause—What Can I Do?—The Individual Value of each Man's Help—The Weak and Strong alike bound to Labour—Neutrality a species of Oppression—Every Man has a Life-Task allotted to him.

I.

BROWN Autumn cometh, with her liberal hand
    Binding the Harvest in a thousand sheaves:
A yellow glory brightens o'er the land,
    Shines on thatched corners and low cottage-eaves,
    And gilds with cheerful light the fading leaves:
Beautiful even here, on hill and dale;
    More lovely yet where Scotland's soil receives
The varied rays her wooded mountains hail,
With hues to which our faint and soberer tints are pale.

II.

For there the Scarlet Rowan seems to mock
    The red sea coral—berries, leaves, and all;
Light swinging from the moist green shining rock
    Which beds the foaming torrent's turbid fall;
    And there the purple cedar, grandly tall,
Lifts its crowned head and sun-illumined stem;
    And larch (soft drooping like a maiden's pall)
Bends o'er the lake, that seems a sapphire gem
Dropt from the hoary hill's gigantic diadem.

III.

And far and wide the glorious heather blooms,
　Its regal mantle o'er the mountains spread;
Wooing the bee with honey-sweet perfumes,
　By many a viewless wild flower richly shed;
　Up-springing 'neath the glad exulting tread
Of eager climbers, light of heart and limb;
　Or yielding, soft, a fresh elastic bed,
When evening shadows gather, faint and dim,
And sun-forsaken crags grow old, and gaunt, and grim.

IV.

Oh, Land! first seen when Life lay all unknown,
　Like an unvisited country o'er the wave,
Which now my travelled heart looks back upon,
　Marking each sunny path, each gloomy cave,
　With here a memory, and there a grave:—
Land of romance and beauty; noble land
　Of Bruce and Wallace; land where, vainly brave,
Ill-fated Stuart made his final stand,
Ere yet the shivered sword fell hopeless from his hand—

V.

I love you! I remember you! though years
　Have fleeted o'er the hills my spirit knew,
Whose wild uncultured heights the plough forbears,
　Whose broomy hollows glisten in the dew.
　Still shines the calm light with as rich a hue
Along the wooded valleys stretched below?
　Still gleams my lone lake's unforgotten blue?
Oh, land! although unseen, how well I know
The glory of your face in this autumnal glow!

VI.

I know your deep glens, where the eagles cry;
　I know the freshness of your mountain breeze,
Your brooklets, gurgling downward ceaselessly,
　The singing of your birds among the trees,
　Mingling confused a thousand melodies!

I know the lone rest of your birchen bowers,
  Where the soft murmur of the working bees
Goes droning past, with scent of heather flowers,
And lulls the heart to dream even in its waking hours.

VII.

I know the grey stones in the rocky glen,
  Where the wild red-deer gather, one by one,
And listen, startled, to the tread of men
    Which the betraying breeze hath backward blown!(21)
    So,—with such dark majestic eyes, where shone
Less terror than amazement,—nobly came
    Peruvia's Incas,(22) when, through lands unknown,
The cruel conqueror with the blood-stained name
Swept, with pursuing sword and desolating flame!

VIII.

So taken, so pursued, so tracked to death,
  The wild free monarch of the hills shall be,
By cunning men, who creep, with stifled breath,
    O'er crag and heather-tuft, on bended knee,
    Down-crouching with most thievish treachery;
Climbing again, with limbs o'erspent and tired,
    Watching for that their failing eyes scarce see,—
The moment, long delayed and long desired,
When the quick rifle-shot in triumph shall be fired.

IX.

Look! look!—what portent riseth on the sky?
  The glory of his great betraying horns;
Wide-spreading, many-branched, and nobly-high,
  (Such spoil the chieftain's hall with pride adorns.)
  Oh, Forest-King! the fair succeeding morns
That brighten o'er those hills, shall miss your crest
  From their sun-lighted peaks! He's hit,—but scorn
To die without a struggle: sore distrest,
He flies, while daylight fades, receding in the West.

X.

Ben-Doran(23) glows like iron in the forge,
    Then to cold purple turns, — then gloomy grey;
And down the ravine-pass and mountain-gorge
    Scarce glimmers now the faintest light of day.
    The moonbeams on the trembling waters play,
(Though still the sky is flecked with bars of gold;)
    And there the noble creature stands, at bay;
His strained limbs shivering with a sense of cold,
While weakness films the eye that shone so wildly bold.

XI.

His fair majestic head bows low at length;
    And, leaping at his torn and bleeding side,
The fierce dogs pin him down with grappling strength;
    While eager men come on with rapid stride,
    And cheer, exulting in his baffled pride.
Now, from its sheath drawn forth, the gleaming knife
    Stabs his broad throat: the gaping wound yawns wide:
One gurgling groan, the last deep sigh of life,
Wells with his gushing blood, — and closed is all the strife!

XII.

'Tis done! The hunted, animal Despair,
    That hoped and feared no future state, is past:
O'er the stiff nostril blows the evening air;
    O'er the glazed eye real darkness gathers fast;
    Into a car the heavy corse is cast;
And homeward the belated hunter hies,
    Eager to boast of his success at last,
And shew the beauty of his antlered prize,
To Her he loves the best, — the maid with gentle eyes!

XIII.

And she, whose tender heart would beat and shrink
    At the loud yelping of a punished hound,
With rosy lips and playful smile shall drink
    The Highland health to him, that circles round.
    And where the creature lies, with crimson wound,

And cold, stark limbs, and purple eyes half-closed,
 There shall her gentle feet at morn be found!
Of such strange mixtures is the heart composed,
So natural-soft,—so hard, by cunning CUSTOM glozed.

XIV.

But, lo! the Sabbath rises o'er those hills!
 And gathering fast from many a distant home,
By wild romantic paths, and shallow rills,
 The Highland groups to distant worship come.
 Lightly their footsteps climb, inured to roam
Miles through the trackless heather day by day:
 Lasses, with feet as white as driven foam,
And lads, whose various tartans, brightly gay,
With shifting colour deck the winding mountain way.

XV.

And some, with folded hands and looks demure,
 Are nathless stealing lingering looks behind,
Their young hearts not less reverently pure
 Because they hope to welcome accents kind,
 And, in that Sabbath crowd, the Loved to find;
And children, glancing with their innocent eyes,
 At every flower that quivers in the wind;
And grey-haired shepherds, calm, and old, and wise,
With peasant-wisdom,—drawn from gazing on the skies.

XVI.

And Auld-Wives, who with Sabbath care have donned
 Their snowy mutches, clean, and fresh, and white;
And pious eyes that well The BOOK have conned;
 And snooded heads, bound round with ribands bright;
 And last,—an old man's grandchild, treading light
By his blind footsteps; or a Mother mild,
 Whose shadowy lashes veil her downcast sight,
Bearing along her lately christened child:—
And still by friendly talk their journey is beguiled.

XVII.

Oh, Scotland, Scotland!—in these later days,
　How hath thy decent worship been disgraced!
Where, on your Sabbath hills, for prayer and praise,
　Solemn the feet of reverend elders paced,
　With what wild brawling, with what ruffian haste,
Gathering to brandish Discord's fatal torch,
　Have men your sacred altar-grounds defaced;
Mocking with howling fury, at the porch,
The ever-listening God, in his own holy Church!(24)

XVIII.

The Taught would choose their Teacher: be it so!
　Doubtless his lessons they will humbly learn,
Bowing the meek heart reverently low,
　Who first claim right to choose him or to spurn;
　Drop sentences of suffrage in the urn;
And ballot for that Minister of God,
　Whose sacred mission is to bid them turn
Obedient eyes toward the chastening rod,
And walk the narrow path by humbler Christians trod!

XIX.

Choose,—since your forms permit that choice to be,—
　But choose in brotherhood, and pious love;
Assist at that selection solemnly,
　As at a sacrifice to One above.
　What! fear ye Rome's high altars? Shall THEY prove
The error and the stumbling-block alone?
　Their crucifixes, meant your hearts to move,—
Their pictured saints—their images of stone—
Their Virgins garlanded—their Jesu on his Throne?

XX.

Yea! rather fear "the image of a Voice,"(25)
　Set up to be an idol and a snare:
Fear the impression of your prideful choice,
　The human heart-beat mingling with the prayer;
　The heavy sigh that comes all unaware;

The sense of weeping, strugglingly represt;
   The yearning adoration and despair,
With which unworthiness is then confest;
Mortal disturbance sent to break Religion's rest!

XXI.

Fear the excitement—fear the human power
   Of eloquent words, which 'twixt you and the skies,
Stand like a fretted screen; and, for that hour,
   Confuse and mar the tranquil light that lies
   Beyond, unbroken! Fear the glow that dies
With the occasion: darkest dangers yawn
   'Neath the foundation where your hope would rise:
For true light fadeth not, nor is withdrawn,
The Lamb's calm City wrapt in one Eternal Dawn!(26)

XXII.

Children, who playing in their ignorant mirth,
   Behold the sunbeam's warm reflected ray,
Reaching to grasp it, touch the blank cold earth,
   Their eyes averted from the Source of Day,
   Not knowing where the Actual Glory lay.
Fear YE to snatch at glittering beams, and lose
   The light that should have cheered your mortal way:
Tremble, responsible yet weak, to choose;
"Ye know not what ye ask,"—nor what ye should refuse!

XXIII.

Say, was it word of power, or fluent speech,
   Which marked those simple men of Galilee,
For Christ's disciples? was it theirs to preach
   With winning grace, and artful subtilty,
   The Saviour's message,—"Die to live with me?"
Bethsaida's fisherman, who bare the spite
   Of heathen rage at Patras,—or those three
Who saw HIM glorified on Tabor's height,
And bathed in bloody sweat on dark Gethsemane's night?(27)

XXIV.

The homeliest voice that weakly leads the van
   Of many prayers, shall sound as sweet among
The angel host,—as his, the eloquent man,
      Who with miraculous sweet, and fervent tongue,
      Charms with a spell the mute, applauding throng;
No better, (as respects his human gift)
      Than many a Heathen Poet, whose great song,
   Age after age continues yet to lift,
As down the Stream of Time melodious treasures drift.

XXV.

Brothers, why make ye War? and in His Name,
   Whose message to the earth was Peace and Love;(28)
What time the awful voice to Shepherds came,
      And the clear Herald-Star shone out above?
      When shall the meaning of that message move
Our bitter hearts? When shall we cease to come
   The patience of a gentle God to prove;
   Cainlike in temper,—though no life we doom,—
Our prayer a curse, although our altar be no tomb?

XXVI.

When that indulgence which the PERFECT grants,
   By the IMPERFECT also shall be granted;
When narrow light that falls in crooked slants,
      Shines broad and bright where'er its glow is wanted;
      When cherished errors humbly are recanted;
When there are none who set themselves apart,
      To watch how Prayers are prayed, and sweet hymns chanted;
   With eyes severe, and criticising heart,—
As though some Player flawed the acting of his part.

XXVII.

From Saints on Earth,—defend us, Saints in Heaven!
   By their un-likeness to the thing they ape;
Their cheerlessness, where God such joy hath given,
      (Covering this fair world with a veil of crape)
      Their lack of kindliness in any shape;

Their fierce, false judgments of another's sin;
   And by the narrowness of mind they drape
With full-blown fantasies, and boasts to win
A better path to Heaven, than others wander in!

XXVIII.

And ye, calm Angels in that blissful world,
   From whence (close knit in brotherhood of strife)
The strong rebellious spirits, downward hurled,
   Came to this Earth, with love and beauty rife,
   And poisoned all the fountain-wells of life;
Spread the soft shelter of your peaceful wings,
   When hard looks stab us like a two-edged knife,
And hearts that yearned for Pity's healing springs,
Are mocked, in dying thirst, by gall which Malice brings.

XXIX.

From the cold glare of their self-righteous eyes, —
   From scornful lips, brimful of bitter words, —
From the curled smile that triumphs and defies, —
   From arguments that sound like clashing swords, —
   Save us, ye dwellers among music-chords!
Whose unseen presence doubtless lingers nigh,
   Although no more our blinded sense affords
Your radiant image to the craving eye,
Nor sees your herald-wings, swift-spreading, cleave the sky!

XXX.

No more to Ishmael's thirst, or Hagar's prayer,
   The suffering or the longing heart on Earth;
No more to soothe funereal despair;
   No more to fill the cruise in bitter dearth,
   Or turn the widow's wailing into mirth;
Shall they return who watched in holy pain
   The Human Death, that closed the Heavenly Birth!
Rebellious earth, twice sanctified in vain,
Lonely from those pure steps must evermore remain.

XXXI.

But deep in each man's heart, some angel dwells,—
    Mournfully, as in a sepulchral tomb;
Set o'er our nature like calm sentinels,
    Denying passage to bad thoughts that come
    Tempting us weakly to our final doom,
Patient they watch, whatever may betide;
    Shedding pure rays of glory through the gloom,
And bowing meek wings over human pride,—
As once in the lone grave of Him, the Crucified!

XXXII.

Angels of Grief,—who, when our weak eyes tire
    Of shedding tears, their sad sweet lessons teach;
Angels of Hope,—who lift with strong desire
    Our mortal thoughts beyond a mortal reach;
    Angels of Mercy,—who to gentle speech,
And meek, forgiving words, the heart incline,
    Weaving a link of brotherhood for each;
Angels of Glory,—whose white vestments shine
Around the good man's couch, in dying life's decline.

XXXIII.

Need of such heavenly counterpoise have we
    To bear us up, when we would grovel down;
To keep our clogged and tarnished natures free
    From the world-rust that round our hearts hath grown
    Like mouldering moss upon a sculptured stone;
To soften down the cruelty and sin
    Of crabbèd Selfishness, that stands alone,
With greedy eyes that watch what they may win,
The whole wide world a field to gather harvest in!

XXXIV.

To gather Harvest! In this Autumn prime,
    Earth's literal harvest cumbers the glad land!
This is the sultry moment—the dry time,
    When the ripe golden ears, that shining stand,
    Fall, rustling, to the Reaper's nimble hand:

When, from those plains the bright sheaves lie among,
   (Whose fertile view the sloping hills command,)
Float cheerful sounds of laughter and of song,
And merry-making jests from many a rural throng.

XXXV.

Sweet is the prospect which that distance yields!
   Here, honest toil;—while there a sunburnt child
Sleeps by the hedge-row that divides the fields,
   Or where the sheltering corn is stacked and piled;
   And as the groups have one by one defiled,
(Leaving unwatched the little sleeper's place,)
   You guess the Mother, by the way she smiled;
The holy Love that lit her peasant-face,
The lingering glance, replete with Feeling's matchless grace.

XXXVI.

He lieth safe until her task be done—
   Lulled, basking, into slumber sound and deep;
That Universal Cherisher, the Sun,
   With kindly glow o'erlooks his harmless sleep,
   And the rough dog close neighbourhood shall keep,
(Friend of the noble and the lowly born)
   Till careful shepherds fold the wandering sheep,
And wearied reapers leave the unfinished corn—
Resting through dewy night, to recommence at morn.

XXXVII.

Oh, picture of Abundance and of Joy!
   Oh, golden Treasure given by God to Man!
Why com'st thou shaded by a base alloy?
   What root of evil poisons Nature's plan?
   Why should the strain not end as it began,
With notes that echo music as they come?
   What mournful silence—what mysterious ban—
Hushes the tones of those who onward roam,
With choral gladness singing,—"happy Harvest-Home?"

XXXVIII.

What altered cadence lingers in the Vale,
　　Whose mass of full-eared sheaves the reapers bind?
A sound more sad than Autumn-moaning gale,
　　More dreary than the later whistling wind
　　That ushers Winter, bitter and unkind.
Again!—it soundeth like a human sigh!
　　A horrid fear grows present to my mind:
Here, where the grain is reaped that stood so high,
A Man hath lain him down: to slumber?—no,—to die!

XXXIX.

Past the Park gate,—along the market-road,—
　　And where green water-meadows freshly shine,
By many a Squire and Peer's unseen abode,—
　　And where the village Alehouse swings its sign,
　　Betokening rest, and food, and strengthening wine,—
By the rich dairy, where, at even-tide,
　　Glad Maidens, singing, milk the lowing kine,—
Under blank shadowing garden-walls, that hide
The espaliered fruit well trained upon their sunnier side,—

XL.

Jaded and foot-sore, he hath struggled on,
　　Retracing with sunk heart his morning track;(29)
In vain to HIM the Harvest and the Sun;
　　Doomed, in the midst of plenteousness, to lack,
　　And die unfed, beneath the loaded stack,
He hath been wandering miles to seek RELIEF;
　　(Disabled servant—Labour's broken hack!)
And he returns—refused! His Hour is brief;
But there are those at home for whom he groans with grief.

XLI.

My pulse beats faster with the coming fear!
　　I cannot lift his dull expiring weight:
What if the fainting wretch should perish here?
　　Here,—sinking down beside the rich man's gate,—
　　On the cropped harvest;—miserable fate!

He tells me something—what, I cannot learn:
    Feeble—confused—the words he fain would state:
But accents of complaint I can discern,
And mention of his wife and little ones in turn!

XLII.

He's DEAD! In that last sigh his weak heart burst!
    An end hath now been put to many woes:
The storm-beat mariner hath reached the worst,—
    His "harbour and his ultimate repose."(30)
    He to a world of better justice goes,
We to the Inquest-Room, to hear, in vain,
    Description of the strong convulsive throes,
The mighty labour, and the petty gain,
By which a struggling life gets quit at last of pain.

XLIII.

To hear, and to forget, the oft-told story,
    Of what forsaken Want in silence bears:
So tarnishing commercial England's glory!
    To hear rich men deny that poor men's cares
    Should be accounted business of theirs;
To hear pale neighbours (one degree less poor
    Than him who perished) prove, all unawares,
The generous opening of THEIR lowly door,
The self-denying hearts that shared the scanty store.(31)

XLIV.

To hear, and acquiesce in, shallow words,
    Which make it seem the sickly labourer's fault,
That he hath no accumulated hoards
    Of untouched wages; wine, and corn, and malt;
    To use when eyesight fails, or limbs grow halt;
To hear his character at random slurred,—
    "An idle fellow, sir, not worth his salt;"
And every one receive a bitter word
For whom his clay-cold heart with living love was stirred:

XLV.

His Wife, a shrew and slattern, knowing not
   (What all her betters understand so well)
How to bring comfort to a poor man's lot,
    How to keep house,—and how to buy and sell;
    His Daughter, a degraded minx, who fell
At sixteen years,—and bore a child of shame,
    Permitted with th' immoral set to dwell!
His eldest Son, an idiot boy, and lame,—
In short, the man WAS starved—but no one was to blame.

XLVI.

No one:—Oh! "Merry England," hearest thou?
   Houseless and hungry died he on thy breast!
No one: Oh! "Fertile England," did thy plough—
    Furrow no fields; or was their growth represt
    By famine-blights that swept from east to west?
No one:—"Religious England," preach the word
   In thy thronged temples on the Day of Rest,
And bid the war of Faith and Works accord:—
"Who giveth to the Poor, he lendeth to the Lord!"

XLVII.

Trust me, that not a soul whose idle hand
   Stinted to spare, and so declined to save;
Not one of all who call it "Native Land,"
    Which to their dead and starved compatriot gave
    A humble cradle,—and a lowlier grave,—
Stands blameless of this death before the face
   Of judging Heaven! The gathered store they have,
That shall condemn them. National disgrace
Rests on the country cursed by such a piteous case.

XLVIII.

And yet not once, nor twice, but countless times,
   We, in blind worship of the golden calf,
Allow of deaths like these! While funeral chimes
    Toll for the rich, whose graven paragraph
    Of vanished virtues (too complete by half),

The heirs of their importance soothe and please.
    The poor man dies—and hath no EPITAPH!
What if your churchyards held such lines as these,
The listless eye to strike,—the careless heart to freeze?

XLIX.

"Here lies a man who died of Hunger-pain,
    In a by-street of England's Capital.
Honest, (in vain!) industrious, (in vain!)
    Willing to spend in useful labour all
    His years from youth to age. A dangerous fall
Shattered his limbs, and brought him to distress.
    His health returned: his strength was past recall:
He asked assistance (earnings growing less,)
Received none, struggled on, and died of Want's excess."(32)

L.

"Here rests in Death, (who rested not in Life!)
    The worn-out Mother of a starving brood:
By night and day, with most courageous strife,
    She fought hard Fortune to procure them food:
    (A desert-pelican, whose heart's best blood
Oozed in slow drops of failing strength away!)
    Much she endured; much misery withstood;
At length weak nature yielded to decay,
And baffled Famine seized his long-resisting prey."(33)

LI.

Oh! the green mounds, that have no head-stones o'er them,
    To tell who lies beneath, in slumber cold;
Oh! the green mounds, that saw no Mutes deplore them,
    The Pauper-Graves, for whom no church-bells tolled;
    What if our startled senses could behold,
(As we to Sabbath-prayer walk calmly by,)
    Their visionary epitaphs enrolled;
Upstanding grimly 'neath God's equal sky,
Near the white sculptured tombs where wealthier Christians lie!

LII.

Then we should THINK: then we should cry, ALAS!
    Then many a pulse would flutter mournfully,
And steps would pause, that now so reckless pass:
    For, in this chequered world of ours, we see
    Much Carelessness, but little Cruelty;
And (though Heaven knows it is no boast to tell,)
    There dwelleth in us a deep sympathy,
Too often, like the stone-closed Arab well,(34)
Sealed from their helpless thirst whose torments it should quell.

LIII.

We shelter SELFISHNESS behind the mask
    Of INCREDULITY: we will not own
What, if admitted, leaves a heavy task
    To be performed; or spurned if left undone,
    Stamping our frozen hearts as made of stone.
Or, if we grant such suffering exists,
    Wide-spread and far, we plead, — "how vain for ONE
To strive to clear away these hopeless mists,
"Striking a few sad names from off these endless lists!"

LIV.

"WHAT CAN I DO? I know that men have died
    "Of their privations; truly, I believe
"That honest labour may be vainly plied:
    "But how am I this sorrow to relieve?
    "Go, let our Rulers some great plan achieve,
"It rests with These to settle and command, —
    "We, meaner souls, can only sigh and grieve."
So, sitting down, with slack and nerveless hand,
Supine we hear the cry that waileth through the land.

LV.

But let us measure help, by their deep woe:
    Are we, indeed, as powerless to aid
As they to struggle? Conscience whispers, "NO!"
    Conscience, who shrinks uneasy and afraid,
    Condemned, — if that brief answer must be made.

Though, in the Cowardice that flies the pain,
    A spark of better nature is betrayed,
Proving, if their appeal could entrance gain,
Our hearts would not be roused and spoken to in vain.

LVI.

But because generous minds stand few and far,
    Like wholesome ears of grain in fields of blight: —
Because one earnest soul, like one great star,
    Rises, — without the power in single light
    To break the darkness of surrounding night: —
Because the sufferings of the Mass require
    The Many, not the Few, their wrongs to right;-
Therefore, Great Hearts grow sick with vain desire,
And, baffled at each turn, the weaker spirits tire.

LVII.

The GRADUAL is God's law. And we all fail
    Because we will not copy it, but would
Against deep-rooted obstacles prevail,
    (Which have the change of centuries withstood)
    By hurried snatching in our rashest mood:
So, leaving dying branches in our grasp,
    Vanishes all the growth of promised good;
Or from the green leaves darts some poisonous asp,
And stings the hand outstretched the fruitage fair to clasp.

LVIII.

So the Mock-Patriot leaves the Poor man's home
    A thousand times more wretched, than when first
Loud declamation, full of froth and foam,
    Weak discontent to strong rebellion nurst!
    By those to whom he proffered aid, accurst, —
Called to account for days of helpless woe, —
    The bubble promises give way, and burst,
Which left his rash lips with such ready flow:
The Idol of Himself, — the Orator for show!

LIX.

Solemn the malediction set on him
   Who doth "pervert the judgment" of the poor,(35)
Mislead the blind and ignorant, and dim
   The meagre light which led them heretofore.
   Faces he knows not,—weak ones who deplore
The ruin wrought by him,—in dreams shall rise;
   Night's veil of darkness cannot cover o'er
The wild reproaching of their blood-shot eyes,
Nor its deep silence hush their hoarse lamenting cries!

LX.

While those whom he opposed, pronounce it Sin,
   That, with mad Discord in his meteor track,
Some shallow theory of hope to win,
   He hounded on a wild infuriate pack:
   The feet he taught to leave the quiet track,
Who shall prevent, or whither shall they tread?
   What mighty force shall dam the waters back,
When the swoln torrent hath found room to spread?
Rolling and fierce it comes, and whelms his reckless head!

LXI.

Yet, let no man who feels himself secure
   That Wrong exists, believe that humble tools
May not amend, what pining they endure.
   Let him not fear the ridicule of fools,
   Nor sneers of cold utilitarian schools,
To whom enthusiasts ever seem insane:
   Nor to old laws and inappropriate rules
Bow slavish down because his lot is plain,
Unstarred by Rank or Power, ungilt by Wealth or Gain.

LXII.

What! were they demi-gods and angels, then,
   Who have done deeds of glory in our land?
Or only honest, earnest-hearted men,
   Born their great mission here to understand,
   And nobly labour at it, heart and hand?

Were they all Princes and great Lords, who trod
    Their share of Earth in natural command?
No! THEY believed the Breath that woke the clod,
And honoured in themselves the sentient spark from God!

LXIII.

HE did not breathe a different breath of life
    Into the noble and the lowly born:
Sprung from one clay, though now in parted strife,
    Brothers,—though some may crouch and some may scorn.
    WE framed a difference, such as bids the Morn
Shine veiled or bright; but, sent through latticed pane,
    Or mullioned arch, or prison-bars forlorn,
Or gleaming through dim aisles with painted stain,
God's outward light it was, God's light it must remain!

LXIV.

Not in the body, or the body's gauds,—
    Not in the coronet a goldsmith wrought,—
Not in the pomp a gaping crowd applauds
    (Like a pleased child when spangled toys are brought,)
    But in the proud pre-eminence of THOUGHT
Lies the true influence that shall aspire:
    The Victory in a battle mutely fought:
For that light, none can trample out,—that fire
The breath of fierce disdain but teaches to rise higher!

LXV.

Hath Science, in her march, avowed no claims
    But theirs, first trained in Academic letters?
Doth History give no roll of patriot-names,
    Peasants themselves, of peasant sons begetters,
    Who taught that light to some, miscalled their BETTERS?
Men, who with iron hands, and hearts as stout,
    Filed through the links of Folly's golden fetters;
And rough smith's work they made of it, no doubt,
Small choice of tools, when Souls from Prison would break out.

LXVI.

Yet doubly beautiful it is to see
    One, set in the temptation of High Class,
Keep the inherent deep nobility
    Of a great nature, strong to over-pass
    The check of circumstance and choking mass
Of vicious faults which youthful leisure woo;
    Mirror each thought in Honour's stainless glass;
And, by all kindly deeds that Power can do,
Prove that the brave good heart hath come of lineage true.

LXVII.

His gladdest welcome shall be giv'n by those
    Who seemed to hold aloof from gentle blood:
Men, falsely deemed RANK'S democratic foes,
    Because they love not FASHION'S selfish brood,
    And look on idle Pomp with bitter mood.
Straightforward is their judgment; true, and keen;
    The English Oak disowns the grafted wood, —
Spurns the high title, linked with spirit mean, —
And scorns the branch whereon the Lowly dare not lean!

LXVIII.

Oh! Graceful seems the bending of his brow;
    Lovely the earnestness that fills his eyes;
Holy the fire that gave his heart its glow
    (Spark of that same great Light which never dies.)
    With hope, not fear, they watch his gradual rise: —
His youth's glad service in his age recall: —
    Cheer in the race, — and glory in the prize, —
For his sake loving Rank, and Pomp, and all, —
Deeming such statue needs a lofty Pedestal!

LXIX.

CHILD OF THE ISLANDS! May such men as these
    Alone be teachers of thy childhood pure;
Greet thy fair youth with friendly courtesies,
    And to thine age with happy bond endure.
    Feel with them; act with them; those ills to cure

That lie within the reach of brotherhood;
    For these are men no shallow hopes allure,
  Whose loyalty is current in their blood,
But who the people's claims have wisely understood.

LXX.

Hear a brief fable. One, with heedless tread,
    Came o'er the wild fair grass that ne'er was mown:
Then said the grass, — "Your heel is on my head;
    And, where in harmless freedom I have grown,
  Sorely your iron foot hath tramped me down;
But God, — who to my veins such freshness gave,
    Shall heal me with a healing of his own,
Till I, perchance, may lift my head to wave
Above the marble tomb that presses down your grave."

LXXI.

If he had trod the path within his reach,
    And let the wild grass hear the cricket sing,
Think you it would have turned with bitter speech?
    No! but saluted him as Nature's king.
    Oh, fable, — but not folly, — for the thing
We trample down, if life from God be in it,
    Sooner or later takes the upward spring;
And sorely we may rue the reckless minute
We strove to crush its strength, and not in peace to win it.

LXXII.

And not alone in this same trampling strife
    Consists Oppression's force; that creeping eft,
That lizard-blooded, frozen death-in-life,
    NEUTRALITY, the cursed of Heaven,(36) hath left
    More misery to be borne by those bereft
Of power to strive against ill-fortune's spite.
    The dagger hath gone home unto the heft;
And those stood by, who would not, but who might
Have turned the assassin steel, and stayed the unequal fight.

LXXIII.

Oh! there are moments of our lives, when such
    As will not help to lift us, strike us down!
When the green bough just bends so near our clutch,
    When the light rope so easily were thrown,
    That they are murderers who behold us drown.
Well spoke the Poet-Heart so tried by woe,(37)
    That there are hours when left despairing, lone,
"Each idle ON-LOOKER appears a FOE:"
For Hate can scarce do worse, than no compassion show.

LXXIV.

Neutrality Is Hate: the aid withheld,
    Flings its large balance in the adverse scale;
And makes the enemy we might have quelled,
    Strong to attack, and certain to prevail;
    Yea, clothes him, scoffing, in a suit of mail!
Those are the days which teach unhappy elves
    No more such callous bosoms to assail;
The rocky soil no more the weak-one delves;
Upright we stand, and trust—in God, and in ourselves.

LXXV.

"The flesh will quiver when the pincers tear;"
    The heart defies, that feels unjustly slighted;
The soul, oppressed, puts off its robe of Fear,
    And warlike stands, in gleaming armour dighted;
    And whensoe'er the Wronged would be the Righted,
There always have been, always must be, minds
    In whom the Power and Will are found united;
Who rise, as Freedom fit occasion finds,
Skilled Workmen in a Craft which no Apprentice binds.

LXXVI.

And therefore should we aid who need our aid,
    And freely give to those who need our giving;
Look gently on a brother's humbler trade,
    And the coarse hand that labours for its living,
    Scorn not because our fortunes are more thriving;

Spurn the cold rule, — "all BARTER, no BESTOWING,"
    And such good plans as answer our contriving,
Let no false shame deter from open shewing; —
The crystal spring runs pure, — though men behold it flowing.

LXXVII.

But granting we in truth were weak to do
    That which our hearts are strong enough to dream;
Shall we, as feeble labourers, wandering go,
    And sit down passive by the lulling stream,
    Or slumber basking in the noon-tide beam?
Shall we so waste the hours without recall,
    Which o'er Life's silent dial duly gleam;
And from red morning to the dewy fall,
Folding our listless hands, pursue no aim at all?

LXXVIII.

Would not the lip with mocking smile be curled,
    If some poor reaper of our autumn corn,
Some hired labourer of the actual world,
    Treated our summons with neglect forlorn;
    Pleading that Heaven, which made him weakly-born,
Had thus excused him from all settled task?
    Should we not answer, with a kind of scorn,
"Do what thou canst, — no more can Reason ask,
But think not, unemployed, in idleness to bask?"

LXXIX.

In Heaven's own land, — the heart, — shall we put by
    All tasks to US allotted and assigned, —
While thus the mote within a Brother's eye
    Clearly we see, but to the beam are blind?
    How can we set that reaper sheaves to bind,
According to his body's strength; yet seek
    Excuse for our soul's indolence to find?
Oh! let the red shame flush the conscious cheek, —
For duties planned by God, NO man was born too weak!

LXXX.

Task-work goes through the world! the fluent River
    Turneth the mill-wheels with a beating sound,
And rolleth onward toward the sea for ever!
    The Sea heaves restless to its shoreward bound;
    The Winds with varying voices, wander round;
The Branches, in their murmur, bend and thrill;
    Flower after flower springs freshly from the ground;
The floating Clouds move ceaseless o'er the hill;
Nothing is set in calm; nothing (save Death) is still.

LXXXI.

That glorious orb of Heaven, the blessèd Sun,
    A daily journey makes from East to West;
Nightly the Moon and Stars their courses run.
    Yea, further we may learn our Lord's behest,
    Taught by the pulse that heaves each living breast,
Our folding of the hands is in the GRAVE
    And fixed in HEAVEN the Sabbath of our Rest!
Meanwhile, with Sun, and Wind, and Cloud, and Wave,
We ply the life-long task our great Creator gave.

LXXXII.

CHILD OF THE ISLANDS! when to thy young heart
    Life's purpose pleads with mighty eloquence, —
Hear, Thou, as one who fain would act his part
    Under the guiding of Omnipotence;
    Whose clay-wrapped Spirit, looking up from hence,
Asketh what labour it may best perform
    Ere the NIGHT cometh; when quick life and sense
Are fellow-sleepers with the slow blind worm, —
And Death's dark curtain hides the sunshine and the storm!

END OF AUTUMN.

WINTER.

THE ARGUMENT.

The Snow on the Graves in the Churchyards of England—The Snow
in Affghanistan—The Soldier's Glory—Arthur Wellesley—Arthur,
Duke of Wellington—Different Destinies—The Worn-out Veteran—
The Blind Man's Winter—Almsgiving—Expensive Pleasures—The
Ballet-Dancer—Christmas Carols—Christmas Privations—Sickness
among the Poor—Kindness of the Poor to each other—Contrast of
the Sick Rich Man and Sick Poor Man—Decline of Life—The Fear
and the Hope of Meeting God—"The Child of the Islands"—His
Share of what Winter brings.

I.

ERE the Night cometh! On how many graves
   Rests, at this hour, their first cold winter's snow!
Wild o'er the earth the sleety tempest raves;
   Silent, our Lost Ones slumber on below;
   Never to share again the genial glow
Of Christmas gladness round the circled hearth;
   Never returning festivals to know,
Or holidays that mark some loved one's birth,
Or children's joyous songs, and loud delighted mirth.

II.

The frozen tombs are sheeted with one pall,—
   One shroud for every churchyard, crisp and bright,—
One foldless mantle, softly covering all
   With its unwrinkled width of spotless white.
   There, through the grey dim day and starlit night,
It rests, on rich and poor, and young and old,—
   Veiling dear eyes,—whose warm homne-cheering light
Our pining hearts can never more behold,—
With an unlifting veil,—that falleth blank and cold.

III.

The Spring shall melt that snow,—but kindly eyes
   Return not with the Sun's returning powers,—

Nor to the clay-cold cheek, that buried lies,
  The living blooms that flush perennial flowers,—
  Nor, with the song-birds, vocal in the bowers,
The sweet familiar tones! In silence drear
  We pass our days,—and oft in midnight hours
Call madly on their names who cannot hear,—
Names graven on the tombs of the departed year!

IV.

There lies the tender Mother, in whose heart
  So many claimed an interest and a share!
Humbly and piously she did her part
  In every task of love and household care:
  And mournfully, with sad abstracted air,
The Father-Widower, on his Christmas Eve,
  Strokes down his youngest child's long silken hair,
And, as the gathering sobs his bosom heave,
Goes from that orphaned group, unseen to weep and grieve.

V.

Feeling his loneliness the more this day
  Because SHE kept it with such gentle joy,
Scarce can he brook to see his children play,
  Remembering how her love it did employ
  To choose each glittering gift and welcome toy:
His little timid girl, so slight of limb,—
  His fearless, glorious, merry-hearted boy,—
They coax him to their sports,—nor know how dim
The Christmas taper's light must burn henceforth for him!

VI.

Ah! when these two are wrapt in peaceful sleep,
  His worn eyes on the sinking embers set,
A Vigil to her Memory shall keep!
  Her bridal blush when first his love she met,—
  Her dying words of meek and fond regret,—
Her tearful thanks for all his kindness past,—
  These shall return to him,—while linger yet
The last days of the year,—that year the last
Upon whose circling hours her sunny smile was cast!

VII.

Life's Dial now shows blank, for want of HER:
    There shall be holiday and festival,
But each his mourning heart shall only stir
    With repetitions of her funeral:
    Quenched is the happy light that used to fall
On common things, and bid them lustre borrow:
    No more the daily air grows musical,
Echoing her soft good night and glad good morrow,
Under the snow she lies,—and he must grieve down sorrow!(38)

VIII.

And learn how Death can hallow trivial things;
    How the eyes fill with melancholy tears
When some chance voice a common ballad sings
    The Loved sang too, in well-remembered years,—
    How strangely blank the beaten track appears
Which led them to the threshold of our door,—
    And how old books some pencilled word endears;
Faint tracery, where our dreaming hearts explore
Their vanished thoughts whose souls commune with us no more!

IX.

Under the snow she lies! And there lies too
    The young fair blossom, neither Wife nor Bride;
Whose Child-like beauty no man yet might woo,
    Dwelling in shadow by her parent's side
    Like a fresh rosebud, which the green leaves hide.
Calm as the light that fades along the West,
    When not a ripple stirs the azure tide,
She sank to Death: and Heaven knows which is best,
The Matron's task fulfilled, or Virgin's spotless rest.

X.

A quiet rest it is: though o'er that form
    We wept, because our human love was weak!
Our Dove's white wings are folded from the storm,—
    Tears cannot stain those eyelids pure and meek,—
    And pale for ever is the marble cheek

Where, in her life, the shy quick-gushing blood
   Was wont with roseate eloquence to speak;
Ebbing and flowing with each varying mood
Of her young timid heart, so innocently good!

XI.

And, near her, sleeps the old grey-headed Sire,
   Whose faded eyes, in dying prayer uplifted,
Taught them the TRUTH who saw him thus expire,
   (Although not eloquent or greatly gifted)
   Because they saw the winnowing fan that sifted
Chaff from the grain, disturbed not his high Trust:
   In the dark storm, Hope's anchor never drifted,
The dread funereal sentence, "Dust to Dust,"
No terror held for him who slumbers with the Just.

XII.

There, too, is laid the son of many vows;
   The stately heir—the treasure of his home:
His early death hath saddened noble brows,
   Yet to grieved hearts doth consolation come:
   Where shall they find, though through the world they roam,
A star as perfect, and as radiant clear?
   Like Ormonde's Ossory,(39) in his early doom,
The throb of triumph checks the rising tear;
No living son can be their dead Son's proud compeer.

XIII.

HE was not called to leave temptations hollow,
   And orgies wild, and bacchanalian nights:
Where vice led on, his spirit scorned to follow:
   His soul, self-exiled from all low delights,
   Mastered the strength of sensual appetites:
Great plans, good thoughts, alone had power to move him,
   Holy Ambition, such as Heaven requites:
His heart, (as they best know who used to love him,)
Was young, and warm, but pure, as the white snow above him.

XIV.

He sleeps! And she, his young betrothèd bride,
   Sleeps too,—her beauty hid in winding-sheet.
The blind tears, freely shed for both, are dried;
   And round their silent graves the mourner's feet
   Have ceased to echo: but their souls shall meet
In the far world, where no sad burial chime
   Knells for departed life; but, endless sweet,
In purity, and love, and joy sublime,
Eternal Hope survives all past decays of Time.

XV.

And there, rests One, whom none on earth remember
   Except that heart whose fond life fed its own!
The cherished babe, who, through this bleak December,
   Far from the Mother's bosom, lieth lone,
   Where the cold North-wind makes its wintry moan.
A flower, whose beauty cannot be renewed;
   A bird, whose song beyond the cloud is gone;
A child, whose empty cradle is bedewed
By bitter-falling tears in hours of solitude!

XVI.

Ah! how can Death untwist the cord of Love,
   Which bid those parted lives together cling?
Prest to the bosom of that brooding Dove,
   Into those infant eyes would softly spring
   A sense of happiness and cherishing:
The tender lips knew no completed word,—
   The small feet could not run for tottering,—
But a glad silent smile the red mouth stirred,
And murmurs of delight whene'er her name was heard!

XVII.

Oh! Darling, since all life for death is moulded,
   And every cradled head some tomb must fill,—
A little sooner only hast thou folded
   Thy helpless hands, that struggled and are still:
   A little sooner thy Creator's will

79

Hath called thee to the Life that shall endure;
    And, in that Heaven his gathered saints shall fill,
Hath "made thy calling and election sure."
His work in thee being done, was thy death premature?

XVIII.

    Baptised,—and so from sin innate reclaimed,—
      Pure from impure,—Redemption's forfeit paid,—
    Too young to be for wilful errors blamed,—
      Thy Angel, little Child so lowly laid,
      For ever looketh upward, undismayed!
    No earthly trespass, clouding Heaven's clear light,
      Casts the Great Glory into dreadful shade:
    We weep for thee by day,—we weep by night,—
Whilst thou beholdest GOD with glad enraptured sight!

XIX.

    Whom call we prematurely summoned? All
      In whom some gleams of quivering sense remain:
    Leaves not quite rotted yellow to their fall,
      Flowers not yet withered dry in every vein:
      All who depart ere stress of mortal pain
    Makes that which crushes pain a blessed boon:
      The extremest verge of life we would attain,—
    And come he morning, evening, night, or noon,
Death, which must come to all, still comes to all too soon.

XX.

    For either,—being young,—a bitter strife
      Divides the parent's heart 'twixt woe and wonder,
    Or, being set and planted in mid-life,
      So many earthward roots are torn asunder,
      The stroke falls blasting like the shock of thunder!
    Or, being old, and good, and fit to die,
      The greater is their loss who sheltered under
    That tree's wide-spreading branches! Still we sigh,
And, craving back our Dead, lament them where they lie!

XXI.

Yet there, the pangs of mortal grief are o'er!
    Pictures and lockets worn in Love's wild fever,
Rest on unthrobbing hearts: ears hear no more
    Harsh words, which uttered once must haunt for ever,
    Despite forgiving wish, and sad endeavour:—
Maniacs, whom fellow-creatures feared and bound,
    Learn the dread fastening of their chain to sever;
Those bloodshot eyes, that glared so wildly round,
Sealed in eternal calm, and closed in holy ground.

XXII.

Peace comes to those, who, restless and forlorn,
    Wasting in doubt's cold torment, day by day,
Watched alienated eyes for fond return
    Of Love's warm light for ever passed away.
    Ah, fools! no second morn's renewing ray
Gilds the blank Present, like the happy Past;
    Madly ye built, 'mid ruin and decay,—
Striving Hope's anchor in the sand to cast,
And, drifting with the storm, made shipwreck at the last!

XXIII.

There your Philosophers and Poets dwell:
    Your great Inventors,—men of giant mind;
The hearts that rose with such a mighty swell,
    How little earth sufficeth now to bind!
    Heroes and Patriots, Rulers of their kind,
Ambitious Statesmen, flatterers of the Throne,
    All, in this lowly rest, their level find:
The weakness of their mortal strength laid down
Beneath the mouldering leaves of Glory's laurelled crown.

XXIV.

And high above them, on the cypress bough,
    The little winter robin, all day long,
Slanting his bright eye at the dazzling snow,
    Sings with a loud voice and a cheerful song:
    While round about, in many a clustering throng,

The tufted snowdrop lifts its gentle head,
    And bird and flower, in language mute yet strong,
Reprove our wailing for the happy dead,
And, by their joy, condemn the selfish tears we shed.

XXV.

For Snowdrops are the harbingers of Spring, —
    A sort of link between dumb life and light, —
Freshness preserved amid all withering, —
    Bloom in the midst of grey and frosty blight, —
    Pale Stars that gladden Nature's dreary night!
And well the Robin may companion be,
    Whose breast of glowing red, like embers bright,
Carries a kindling spark from tree to tree,
Lighting the solemn yew where darkness else would be.

XXVI.

The Rose is lovely fair, and rich in scent,
    The Lily, stately as a cloistered nun,
The Violet, with its sweet head downward bent,
    The Polyanthus, in the noon-day sun,
    And Blue-bell swinging where the brooklets run:
But all these grow in summer hours of mirth;
    Only the Snowdrop cometh forth alone,
Peering above the cold and niggard earth,
Then bending down to watch the soil that gave it birth.

XXVII.

Seeming to say, — "Behold, your DEAD lie here,
    "Beneath the heavy mould whose burial sound
"Smote with such horror on your shrinking ear
    "When the dark coffin sank beneath the ground:
    "Yet therefrom spring these flowers that quiver round,
"Their frail bells trembling o'er the damp cold sod.
    "Fear not, nor doubt—your lost ones shall be found;
"For they, like us, shall burst the valley clod,
"And, in white spotless robes, rise up to light and God!"

XXVIII.

Oh! nothing cheerless dwelleth by the tomb,
  And nothing cheerless in the wintry sky;
They are asleep whose bed is in that gloom;
  They are at rest who in that prison lie,
  And have no craving for their liberty!
They hear no storm; the clear frost chills them not,
  When the still solemn stars shine out on high;
The dreamless slumber of the grave shall blot
All record of dull pain and suffering from their lot!

XXIX.

Theirs was the Dreadful Snow,—who, hand to hand,
  Bravely, but vainly, massacre withstood,
In the dark passes of the INDIAN land,
  Where thoughts of unforgotten horror brood!
  Whose cry for mercy, in despairing mood,
Rose in a language foreign to their foes,(40)
  Groaning and choking in a sea of blood,
No prayer—no hymn to soothe their last repose,
No calm and friendly hands their stiffening eyes to close!

XXX.

Theirs was the Dreadful Snow,—who trembling bore
  Their shuddering limbs along; and pace by pace
Saw in that white sheet plashed with human gore
  The dread familiar look of some brave face,—
  Distorted,—ghastly,—with a lingering trace
Of life and sorrow in its pleading glance,—
  A dying dream of parted Love's embrace,—
A hope of succour, brought by desperate chance,—
Or wild unconscious stare of Death's delirious trance.

XXXI.

Theirs was the Dreadful Snow,—who left behind
  Brothers and husbands, foully, fiercely slain:
Who, led by traitors, wandered on, half blind
  With bitter tears of sorrow, shed in vain,
  Crossing the steep ascent, or dreary plain;

Mothers of helpless children,—delicate wives,
　　Who brought forth wailing infants, born in pain,
　　Amid a crowded wreck of human lives,
And scenes that chill the soul, though vital strength survives.(41)

XXXII.

Theirs was the Dreadful Snow,—who never laid
　　Their Dead to rest with service and with psalm:
Their bones left bleaching in the alien shade
　　Of mountains crested with the Indian Palm.
　　Oh! English village graves, how sweet and calm
Shines on your native earth the setting sun!
　　Yet GLORY gave their wounds a healing balm—
Glory,—like that thy youthful trophies won
In thy first "prime of life,"—(42) victorious Wellington!

XXXIII.

"In thy life's prime,"—ere yet the fading grey
　　Had blanched the tresses of thy gallant head:
Or from thy step Time's gradual faint decay
　　Stole the proud bearing of a Soldier's tread!
　　Gone are the troops thy voice to battle led,—
Thy conquering hand shall wield the sword no more,—
　　The foes and comrades of thy youth are dead,—
By Elba's rock and lone St. Helen's shore
No prisoned Emperor hears the boundless ocean roar.

XXXIV.

But, though its battle-strength be out of date,
　　The eager gesture of that warrior hand,—
Raised in the warmth of brief and blunt debate
　　In the hushed Senate of thy native land,—
　　Hath something in it of the old command;(43)
The voice retains a certain power to thrill
　　Which cheered to Victory many a gallant band:
In thy keen sense, and proud unconquered will,
Though thy Life's Prime be past, men own their Leader still!

XXXV.

Plodding his way along the winter path,
   Behold, a different lot hard fortune shews:
A blind old veteran in the tempest's wrath,
   Around whose feet no fabled laurel grows.
   Long hath he dwelt in an enforced repose;
And, when the tales of glorious deeds are heard,
   His sightless countenance with pleasure glows, —
His brave old heart is for a moment stirred, —
Then, sad he shrinks away, muttering some mournful word.

XXXVI.

For ever idle in this work-day world —
   For ever lonely in the moving throng —
Like a seared leaf by eddying breezes whirled,
   Hither and thither vaguely borne along:
   No guide to steer his course, if right or wrong,
Save the dumb immemorial friend of man,
   Who, by some instinct delicate and strong,
From those impassive glances learns to scan
Some wish to move or rest, — some vestige of a plan:

XXXVII.

The wildbird's carol in the pleasant woods
   Is all he knows of Spring! The rich perfume
Of flowers, with all their various scented buds,
   Tells him to welcome Summer's heavy bloom:
   And by the wearied gleaners trooping home, —
The heavy tread of many gathering feet, —
   And by the laden Waggon-loads that come
Brushing the narrow hedge with burden sweet, —
He guesses Harvest in, and Autumn's store complete.

XXXVIII.

But in God's Temple the great lamp is out;
   And he must worship glory in the Dark!
Till Death, in midnight mystery, hath brought
   The veiled Soul's re-illuminating spark, —
   The pillar of the CLOUD enfolds the ark!

And, like a man that prayeth underground
   In Bethlehem's rocky shrine,(44) he can but mark
The lingering hours by circumstance and sound,
And break with gentle hymns the solemn silence round.

XXXIX.

   Yet still Life's Better Light shines out above!
      And in that village church where first he learned
To bear his cheerless doom for Heaven's dear love,
      He sits, with wistful face for ever turned
      To hear of those who Heavenly pity earned:
Blind Bartimeus, and him desolate
      Who for Bethesda's waters vainly yearned:
And inly sighs, condemned so long to wait,
Baffled and helpless still, beyond the Temple gate!

XL.

   And can the Blind man miss the Summer sun?
      This wintry sheet of wide unbroken white
His sealed blank eyes undazzled rest upon;
      Yet round him hangs all day a twofold night,
      He felt the warmth, who never saw the light!
He loved to sit beside the cottage door
      When blossoms of the gorse were golden bright,
And hear glad children's shouts come o'er the moor,
And bask away his time in happy dreams of yore.

XLI.

   The Sunbeam slanting down on bench or bank
      Was, unto him, a sweet consoling friend;
Such as our mournful hearts incline to thank,
      But that such thanks affection's depth offend.
      All vanished pictures it had power to send
That greeted his keen eyesight, long ago!
      Gay plumèd troops defiling without end, —
And glancing bayonets and martial show, —
And hands he used to grasp, —and looks he used to know.

XLII.

Yea, sometimes, back again to earlier life,
    Even to his childish days, his thoughts would steal;
And hear, in lieu of arms and clashing strife,
    The low hum of his Mother's spinning wheel, —
    And on his withered cheek her lips could feel
As when she kissed its boyish sunburnt bloom:
    And fancy little acts of love and zeal,
By which she now would soothe his bitter doom:
But she is dead, —and he, —alone in all his gloom!

XLIII.

Oh! by the beauty of a Summer day, —
    The glorious blue that on the fountain lies, —
The tender quivering of the fresh green spray, —
    The softness of the night when stars arise;
    By the clear gladness of your children's eyes, —
And the familiar sweetness of that face
    Most welcome to you underneath the skies, —
Pity that fellow-creature's mournful case
Whom Darkness follows still, where'er his dwelling-place!

XLIV.

"PITY THE BLIND!" How oft, in dolent tone,
    That cry is heard along the peopled street,
While the Brute-Guide with patient care leads on
    The tardy groping of his Master's feet!
    But little dream we, as those steps we meet,
We too are blind, though clear the visual ray
    That gives us leave familiar looks to greet,
Smiling and pausing on our onward way:
We too are blind, —and dark the paths wherein we stray.

XLV.

Yea, blind! and adder-deaf, —and idiot-dull, —
    To many a sight and sound that cries aloud.
Is there no moral blindness of the Soul?
    Is he less shut from light, who, through the crowd
    Threads his blank way, among the poor and proud, —

The foul and fair,—all forms to him the same,—
　　Than they whose hearts have never yet avowed
Perception of the universal claim
Wrapped in that common phrase, a "fellow-creature's" name.

XLVI.

Christmas is smiling at the Rich man's door,—
　　Its joyolus holiday his home endears:
Christmas is frowning on the thin-clad Poor,
　　With looks of cold distress and frozen tears:
　　How plain the duty of the time appears!
But Selfishness is Blindness of the Heart;
　　And, having eyes, we see not; having ears,
We hear not warnings, which should make us start,
While God's good angels watch the acting of our part.

XLVII.

Now, slowly trudging through the crispèd snow,
　　Under the wintry arch of Heaven's clear dome,
Joy's cadenced music set to tones of woe,
　　Beneath the windows of the rich man's home
　　Street-Singers, with their Christmas Carols, roam.
Ah! who shall recognise that sound again,
　　Nor think of him, who hallowed years to come,
When the past Christmas taught his fervent pen
A "CAROL" of dear love and brotherhood 'twixt men!

XLVIII.

To what good actions that small book gave birth,(45)
　　God only knows, who sends the wingèd seed
To its appointed resting-place on earth!
　　What timely help in hours of sorest need,—
　　What gentle lifting of the bruisèd reed,—
What kind compassion shewn to young and old,—
　　Proved the true learning of its simple creed,—
We know not,—but we know good thoughts, well told,
Strike root in many a heart, and bear a hundred-fold!

XLIX.

Oh, lovely lesson! art thou hard to learn?
  Is it indeed so difficult to share
The school-boy hoard our efforts did not earn?
  Shall we still grudge life's luck, to lives of care,
  And dream that what we spend on these, we spare?
ALMS being the exception, SELF the rule,
  Still shall we give our guinea here and there
("Annual") to church, and hospital, and school,
And lavish hundreds more, on pleasures which befool.

L.

Take but the aggregate of several sums
  Allotted for the privilege to stay,
Watching some dancer's feet, who onward comes
  Light as a bird upon a bending spray:
  When,—oh! thou custom-governed Conscience,—say,
Did niggard Charity at once bestow
  What careless Pleasure squanders every day?
When did the tale of real and squalid woe
Awake within thy breast such sympathetic glow?

LI.

Prosaic Questioner, thy words beguile
  No listener's ear: SHE curtsies, gazing round:
Who would not spend a fortune on her smile!
  How curved the stately form prepared to bound
  With footfall echoing to the music's sound,
In the Cachucha's proud triumphant pace !
  What soft temptation in her look is found
When the gay Tarantalla's wilder grace
Wakes all th' impassioned glow that lights her Southern face!

LII.

And now, a peasant girl, abashed she stands:
  How pretty and how timid are her eyes:
How gracefully she clasps her small fair hands,
  How acts her part of shy and sweet surprise:
  How earnest is her love without disguise:

89

How piteously, when from that dream awaking,
 She finds him false on whom her faith relies,
All the arch mirth those features fair forsaking,
She hides her face and sobs as though her heart were breaking!

LIII.

A Sylphide now, among her bowers of roses,
 Or, by lone reeds, a Lake's enamoured fairy,
Her lovely limbs to slumber she composes,
 Or flies aloft, with gestures soft and airy:
 Still on her guard when seeming most unwary,
Scarce seen, before the small feet twinkle past,
 Haunting, and yet of love's caresses chary,
Her maddened lover follows vainly fast, —
While still the perfect step seems that she danced the last!

LIV.

Poor Child of Pleasure! thou art young and fair,
 And youth and beauty are enchanting things:
But hie thee home, bewitching Bayadère,
 Strip off thy glittering armlets, pearls, and rings,
 Thy peasant boddice, and thy Sylphide wings:
Grow old and starve: require true Christian aid:
 And learn, when real distress thy bosom wrings,
For whom was all that costly outlay made:
For SELF, and not for thee, the golden ore was paid!

LV.

For the quick beating of the jaded heart,
 When sated Pleasure woke beneath thy gaze,
And heaved a languid sigh, alone, apart,
 Half for thy beauty, half for "other days:"
 For the trained skill thy pliant form displays,
Pleasing the eye and casting o'er the mind
 A spell which, Circé-like, thy power could raise,
A drunkenness of Soul and Sense combined,
Where Fancy's filmy Veil gross Passion's form refined.

LVI.

For these, while thou hadst beauty, youth, and health,
  Thou supple-limbed and nimble-stepping slave
Of two cold masters, Luxury and Wealth,
  The wages of thy task they duly gave,
  Thy food was choice, and thy apparel brave:
Appeal not now to vanished days of joy
  For arguments to succour and to save, —
Proud Self indulgence hath a newer toy,
And younger slaves have skill, and these thy Lords employ.

LVII.

And thou, first flatterer of her early prime,
  Ere praises grew familiar as the light,
And the young feet flew round in measured time
  Amid a storm of clapping every night;
  Thou, at whose glance the smile grew really bright
That decked her lips for tutored mirth before, —
  Wilt THOU deny her and forget her quite?
Thy idol, for whose sake the lavish store
In prodigal caprice thy hand was wont to pour?

LVIII.

Yea, wherefore not? for SELF, and not for her,
  Those sums were paid, her facile love to win:
Thy heart's cold ashes vainly would she stir,
  The light is quenched she looked so lovely in!
  Eke out the measure of thy fault, and sin
"First with her, then against her,"(46) cast her off,
  Though on thy words her faith she learned to pin:
The WORLD at her, and not at thee, shall scoff, —
Yea, lowlier than before, its servile cap shall doff.

LIX.

And since these poor forsaken ones are apt
  With ignorant directness to perceive
Only the fact that gentle links are snapt,
  Love's perjured nonsense taught them to believe
  Would last for ever: since to mourn and grieve

Over these broken vows is to grow wild:
   It may be she will come, some winter eve,
   And, weeping like a broken-hearted child,
Reproach thee for the days when she was thus beguiled.

LX.

Then,—in thy spacious library,—where dwell
   Philosophers, Historians, and Sages,
Full of deep lore which thou hast studied well;
   And classic Poets, whose melodious pages
   Are shut, like birds, in lacquered trellis cages,—
Let thy more educated mind explain
   By all experience of recorded ages,
How commonplace is this her frantic pain,
And how such things have been, and must be yet again!

LXI.

If the ONE BOOK should strike those foreign eyes,
   And thy professed Religion she would scan,—
Learning its shallow influence to despise;
   Argue thy falsehood on a skilful plan,
   Protestant, and protesting gentleman!
Prove all the folly, all the fault, her own;
   Let her crouch humbly 'neath misfortune's ban;
She hath unlovely, undelightful grown,
That sin no words absolve: for that no tears atone!

LXII.

But Prudery,—with averted angry glance,—
   Bars pleading, and proclaims the sentence just;
Life's gambler having lost her desperate chance,
   Now let the Scorned One grovel in the dust!
   Now let the Wanton share the Beggar's crust!
Yet every wretch destroyed by Passion's lure,
   Had a First Love,—Lost Hope,—and Broken Trust:
And Heaven shall judge whose thoughts and lives are pure,
Not always theirs worst sin, who worldly scorn endure.

LXIII.

The Worthlessness of those we might relieve
    Is chill Denial's favourite pretence:
The proneness of the needy to deceive
    By many a stale and counterfeit pretence, —
    Their vice, — their folly, — their improvidence.
There's not a ragged beggar that we meet,
    Tuning his voice to whining eloquence,
And shuffling towards us with half-naked feet
As some rich equipage comes rolling down the street, —

LXIV.

But we prepare that Sinner to condemn,
    And speak a curse, where we were called to bless:
From a corrupted root, — a withered stem;
    'Tis gross hypocrisy, and not distress,
    Or want brought on by loathsome drunkenness,
Seen in the wandering of his bloodshot eye
    Glazed stupid with habitual excess:
Even children raise a simulated cry, —
Worthless we deem them all, — and worthless pass them by.

LXV.

Nor without reason is the spirit grieved,
    And wrath aroused for Truth and Justice' sake:
The tales by which vile Cunning hath deceived,
    On calculated chances planned to make
    Frozen Compassion's sealed-up fountains wake;
The affectation of distorted pains;
    The stealthy dram which trembling fingers take
To send the chill blood coursing through the veins
From a worn heart which scarce its vital heat retains; —

LXVI.

Craving of gifts to pawn, exchange, or sell; —
    These are the baser errors of the Poor!
What thine are, Almsgiver, thou best canst tell,
    And how thy spirit its temptations bore,
    Giving thee now a right to bar the door

Against thy fellow-trespasser: his brow
   Hath lost, perchance, the innocence of yore:
The wrestling sin that forced his Soul to bow,
He hath not bravely met and overborne: hast THOU?

LXVII.

Oh, different temptations lurk for all!
   The Rich have idleness and luxury,
The Poor are tempted onward to their fall
   By the oppression of their Poverty:
   Hard is the struggle—deep the agony
When from the demon watch that lies in wait
   The soul with shuddering terror strives to flee,
And idleness—or want—or love—or hate—
Lure us to various crimes, for one condemning fate!

LXVIII.

Didst THOU, when sleety blasts at midnight howled,
   And wretches, clad in Misery's tattered guise,
Like starving wolves, it may be, thieved and prowled;
   Never lie dreaming,—shut from winter skies,—
   While the warm shadow of remembered eyes,
Like a hot sun-glow, all thy frame opprest;
   And love-sick and unhallowed phantasies
Born of a lawless hope, assailed thy breast,
And robbed God's solemn night, of Prayer and tranquil rest.

LXIX.

When the great Sunrise, shining from above
   With an impelling and awakening ray,
Found thee so listless in thy sinful love,
   Thy flushing cheek could only turn away
   From the clear light of that distasteful day,
And, leaning on thy languid hand, invite
   Darkness again, that fading dreams might stay,—
Was God's fair Noon not robbed of Duty's Right,
Even as the holy rest was cheated from his night?

LXX.

Whom thou dost injure,—thou that dost not strike,—
　What thou dost covet,—thou that dost not steal,—
HE knows, who made Temptations so unlike,
　But SIN the same: to HIM all hearts reveal
　The Proteus-like disguises which conceal
That restless Spirit which doth so beguile
　And easily beset us: all we feel
Of good or bad,—He knows,—and all the vile
Degrading earthly stains which secret thought defile.

LXXI.

HIS eye detects the stealthy murderer's arm
　Uplifted in the hour of midnight gloom:
HE sees, through blushes delicately warm,
　Feigned Innocence her forfeit throne resume,
　And marks the canker underneath the bloom:
But oft the sentence erring man decreed,
　Finds before HIM reversal of its doom:
HE judgeth all our sorrow—all our need—
And pitying bends to hear the sorely tempted plead.

LXXII.

What if by HIM more sternly shall be judged
　Crimes to which no necessity impelled,
Than theirs, to whom our human justice grudged
　Compassion for the weeping we beheld?
　What if the savage blow that madly felled
The object of fierce rage, be lighter deemed
　Than cruelty where life-blood never welled,
But where the hope was quenched that faintly gleamed,
And the heart drained of tears which still unpitied streamed?

LXXIII.

What if the village brawl, the drunken bout,
　The Sabbath-breaking of the skittle-ground,
Shall all be sins foregone and blotted out,
　And in their stead worse Sabbath-breaking found
　In that which stands not chid for brawling sound;

The silent printed libel; which invests
    A strip of paper with the power to wound, —
Where some fair name like dew on nightshade rests,
In a coarse gathered heap of foul indecent jests?

LXXIV.

    How, if the ignorant clown less vile appears,
      Than educated stabbers in the dark,
Who joyed in matron grief, and girlish tears,
      And lit in happy homes that quenchless spark
      The bitterness of DOUBT: who bid the ark
Float over troubled waters for all time;
      And those who once sang joyous as the lark
Bow down in silence; tarnished for no crime;
Stung by a trailing snake, and spotted with its slime?

LXXV.

Oh! learnèd, clothed, and cultivated minds,
    To whom the laws their purpose have declared,
Sit ye in judgment but on labouring hinds?
    Yea, for the poor your censure is not spared!
    Yet shall the faults they made, the crimes they dared,
The errors which ye found so hard to pass,
    Seem as the faults of children, when compared
With the corruption of a different class,
When God calls angels forth from this world's buried mass.

LXXVI.

Weigh, weigh and balance nicely as you will
    The poor man's errors with the poor man's need:
The fiat of the Just One liveth still,
    And Human laws, though blindly men may read,
    The law of Heaven can never supersede.
By the cold light of Wisdom's complex rules
    Vainly we study hard a different creed, —
"Do AS YE WOULD BE DONE BY" mocks the schools,
And mars the shallow craft of worldly-witted fools.

LXXVII.

A careless Giver is the poor man's curse!
　　Think not, by this, absolved of alms to stand;
The niggard heart of indolence does worse,
　　Stinting both trouble and the liberal hand.
　　Obey the voice of a divine command;
"Remember Mercy!" haply thou shalt save
　　If only one, of all that mournful band,
From gaol, or workhouse, or an early grave!
Hear, thou,—and Heaven shall hear thy voice for mercy crave.

LXXVIII.

Yea, hear the voice that for compassion calls:
　　Prove him unworthy ere he be denied:
Lest, through thy coldness, dismal workhouse walls
　　Blankly enclose him round on every side,
　　And from his eyes God's outward glory hide.
There, like a creature pent in wooden shed,
　　He in a bitter darkness shall abide,
Duly though sparely clothed, and scantly fed,
But pining for the paths his feet were wont to tread.

LXXIX.

There shall his soul, of Nature's sweetness reft,
　　Robbed of the light that came in angel-gleams
And on the mind such blessed influence left,—
　　Be filled with dark defying prison-dreams.
　　Cruel the world's enforced relieving seems,
Preserving life, but not what made life fair;
　　Stagnant and shut from all life's running streams,
His heart sinks down from feverish restless care,
Into the weary blank of brutalised Despair!

LXXX.

Where is the gorse-flower on the golden moor?
　　Where the red poppy laughing in the corn?
Where the tall lily at the cottage door,—
　　The briar-rose dancing in the breezy morn,—
　　The yellow buttercups of sunshine born,—

The daisies spangling all the village green, —
   The showering blossoms of the scented thorn, —
The cowslips that enwreathed the May-day Queen?
What hath he done, that these shall never more be seen?

LXXXI.

Oh, flowers! oh, dumb companions on lone hills, —
   In meadow walks, and lovely loitering lanes, —
Whose memory brings fresh air and bubbling rills
   Amid Life's suffocating fever-pains;
   For Rich and Poor your equal joy remains!
Decrepid age and childhood's careless mirth
   Alike shall own the power your spell retains:
Midst all the fading changes of the earth
Your smiles, at least, live on, —immortal in their birth.

LXXXII.

Who, when some inward anger fiercely burned, —
   Hath trod the fresh green carpet where ye lie,
Your soft peace-making faces upward turned,
   With a dumb worship to the solemn sky, —
   Nor felt his wrath in shame and sorrow die?
Old voices calling to his haunted heart
   From grassy meadows known in infancy,
Playfields whose memory bids a teardrop start,
Scenes from a former life whose sunshine dwells apart.

LXXXIII. ·

When there had been no quarrels—and no deaths—
   No vacant places in our early home:
When blossoms, with their various scented breaths,
   Were all the pure hearts knew of beauty's bloom,
   Where earthlier passion yet had found no room:
When, from low copse, or sunny upland lawn,
   We shouted loud for joy, that steps might come
Bounding and springing, agile as the fawn, —
And "Sleep came with the dew,"(47) and gladness with the dawn.

LXXXIV.

Oh! Flowers, oh! gentle never-failing friends,
 Which from the world's beginning still have smiled
To cheer Life's pilgrim as he onward wends, —
 Seems not your soothing influence, meek and mild,
 Like comfort spoken by a little child,
Who, in some desperate sorrow, though he knows
 Nothing of all Life's grieving, dark and wild,
An innocent compassion fondly shews,
And fain would win us back from fever to repose?

LXXXV.

For morbid folly let my song be chid, —
 Incur the cynic's proudly withering sneer, —
But these are feelings (unexprest) which bid
 The poor man hold his cottage freedom dear;
 The matin lark hath thrilled his gladdened ear,
With its exulting and triumphant song;
 The nightingale's sweet notes he loved to hear,
In the dim twilight, when the labouring throng
All weary from their work, in silence trudged along.

LXXXVI.

The glowing Claudes, —the Poussins, —which your eyes
 Behold and value, —treasure as you may, —
 His pictures were the sights you do not prize—
The leaf turned yellow by the autumn ray,
 The woodbine wreath that swung across his way,
 The sudden openings in the hazel-wood: —
 He knew no history of Rome's decay,
But, where grey tombstones in the churchyard stood,
He spelt out all the Past on which his mind could brood.

LXXXVII.

Some humble love-scene of his village lot,
 Or some obscure Tradition, could invest
Field, copse, and stile, —or lone and shadowy spot, —
 With all the Poetry his heart confest:
 The old companions that he loved the best

Met not in crowds at Fashion's busy call:
    But loud their merriment, and gay the jest,
At statute fair and homely festival:
And now, life's path is dark, for he hath lost them all!

LXXXVIII.

Therefore deal gently with his destiny,
    Which, rightly looked on, differs from your own,
Less in the points of feeling, than degree:
    Contrast the great and generous pity shewn,—
    The bounteous alms some inquest-hour makes known,—
Bestowed by those whose means of self-support
    Are so precarious,—with the pittance thrown
From niggard hands, which only spend for sport,
Scattering vain largesse down in Pleasure's idle court.

LXXXIX.

Contrast the rich man, with his ready wealth
    Feeing a skilled Physician's hand to ease
The pang that robs him of that blessing Health,
    With the poor man's lone hour of fell disease;
    The wretched ague-fits that burn and freeze,
He understands not; but his aching head
    Is conscious that the wasting arm he sees
Grown daily thinner, earns his children's bread,
And that they pine and starve around his helpless bed.

XC.

Contrast that terror of the chastening rod
    Which those to whom so much was giv'n, must feel,
With the one anxious hope of meeting God!
    Of finding all the bliss, the glory real,—
    The Mercy that their sorrows past shall heal,—
The Eternal rest,—the happy equal share,—
    All that was promised by the Preacher's zeal,
When weekly pausing in a life of care,
Poor voices joined the rich in thanksgiving and prayer.

XCI.

The stamp of imperfection rests on all
    Our human intellects have power to plan;
'Tis Heaven's own mark, fire-branded at the fall,
    When we sank lower than we first began,
    And the Bad Angel stained the heart of man:(48)
The Good our nature struggles to achieve
    Becomes, not what we would, but what we can: —
Ah! shall we therefore idly, vainly grieve,
Or coldly turn away, reluctant to relieve?

XCII.

Even now a Radiant Angel goeth forth,
    A spirit that hath healing on his wings, —
And flieth East and West and North and South
    To do the bidding of the King of Kings:
    Stirring men's hearts to compass better things,
And teaching BROTHERHOOD as that sweet source
    Which holdeth in itself all blessed springs;
And shewing how to guide its silver course,
When it shall flood the world with deep exulting force.

XCIII.

And some shall be too indolent to teach, —
    And some too proud of other men to learn, —
And some shall clothe their thoughts in mystic speech,
    So that we scarce their meaning may discern;
    But all shall feel their hearts within them burn,
(Even those by whom the Holy is denied)
    And in their worldly path shall pause and turn,
Because a Presence walketh by their side,
Not of their earthlier mould, but pure and glorified:

XCIV.

And some shall blindly overshoot the mark,
    Which others, feeble-handed, fail to hit,
And some, like that lone Dove who left the ark,
    With restless and o'erwearied wing to flit
    Over a world by lurid storm-gleams lit, —

Shall seek firm landing for a deed of worth,
  And see the water-floods still cover it:—
For "there are many languages on Earth,
But only one in Heaven," where all good plans have birth.

XCV.

Faint not, oh Spirit, in dejected mood
  Thinking how much is planned, how little done:
Revolt not, Heart, though still misunderstood,
  For Gratitude, of all things 'neath the sun,
  Is easiest lost,—and insecurest, won:
Doubt not, clear mind, that workest out the Right
  For the right's sake: the thin thread must be spun,
And Patience weave it, ere that sign of might,
Truth's Banner, wave aloft, full flashing to the light.

XCVI.

Saw ye the blacksmith with a struggling frown
  Hammer the sparkle-drifting iron straight,—
Saw ye the comely anchor, holding down
  The storm-tried vessel with its shapely weight?
  Saw ye the bent tools, old and out of date,
The crucibles, and fragments of pale ore,—
  Saw ye the lovely coronet of state
Which in the festal hour a monarch wore,
The sceptre and the orb which in her hand she bore?

XCVII.

Saw ye the trudging labourer with his spade
  Plant the small seedling in the rugged ground,—
Saw ye the forest-trees within whose shade
  The wildest blasts of winter wander round,
  While the strong branches toss and mock the sound?
Saw ye the honey which the bee had hived,
  By starving men in desert wandering found;
And how the soul gained hope, the worn limbs thrived,
Upon the gathered store by insect skill contrived?

XCVIII.

Lo! out of Chaos was the world first called,
  And Order out of blank Disorder came.
The feebly-toiling heart that shrinks appalled,
  In Dangers weak, in Difficulties tame,
  Hath lost the spark of that creative flame
Dimly permitted still on earth to burn,
  Working out slowly Order's perfect frame:
Distributed to those whose souls can learn,
As labourers under God, His task-work to discern.

XCIX.

CHILD OF THE ISLANDS! Thou art one by birth
  In whom the weak ones see a human guide:
A Lily in the garden of their earth,
  That toilest not, but yet art well supplied
  With costly luxuries and robes of pride.
Thy word shall lead full many a wavering soul,
  Behoves thee therefore hold thyself allied
With the Mind-Workers, that thy good control
May serve HIS world whose light shines out from pole to pole.

C.

So, when Life's Winter closes on thy toil,
  And the great pause of Death's chill silence comes,—
When seeds of good lie buried in the soil,
  And labourers rest within their narrow homes,—
  When dormant Consciousness no longer roams
In awe-struck fancy towards that distant land
  Where no snow falleth, and no ocean foams,
But waits the trumpet in the Angel's hand,—
THOU may'st be one of those who join Heaven's shining band.

END OF WINTER.

CONCLUSION.

THE ARGUMENT.

"The Child of the Islands" tried by none of the ordinary Grievances of this World—Death of the Duke of Orleans; of the late Daughter of the Emperor Alexander; of the Son of Leopold of Belgium; of Charlotte of England and her Son—The common Brotherhood of Man—Death of two Babes in Opposite Ranks of Life—The Existence of Universal Sympathy a Decree of God—"The Child of the Islands"—The Moral of Greatness by Descent and Heritage—The End.

I.

MY lay is ended! closed the circling year,
    From Spring's first dawn to Winter's darkling night;
The moan of sorrow, and the sigh of fear,
    The ringing chords of triumph and delight
    Have died away,—oh, child of beauty bright,—
And all unconscious of my song art thou:
    With large blue eyes of Majesty and might,
And red full lips, and fair capacious brow,
No Leader of the World,—but Life's Beginner, now!

II.

Oh, tender human blossom, thou art fair,
    With such a beauty as the eye perceives
Watching a bud of promise rich and rare
    In the home-shadow of surrounding leaves.
    THOUGHT, the great Dream-bringer, who joys and grieves
Over the visions of her own creating,
    Resting by Thee, a sigh of pleasure heaves;
The fever of her rapid flight abating
Amid the golden hopes around thy cradle waiting.

III.

Thou—thou, at least, art happy! For thy sake
    Heaven speaks reversal of the doom of pain,
Set on our Nature when the Demon-Snake

Hissed the first lie, a woman's ear to gain,
And Eden was lamented for in vain!
THOU art not meant, like other men, to thirst
For benefits no effort can attain:
To struggle on, by Hope's deceiving nurst,
And linger still the last, where thou wouldst fain be first.

IV.

The royal canopy above thy head
Shall charm away the griefs that others know: —
Oh! mocking dream! Thy feet Life's path must tread:
The Just God made not Happiness to grow
Out of condition: fair the field-flowers blow,
Fair as the richer flowers of garden ground;
And far more equally are joy and woe
Divided, — than they dream, who, gazing round,
See but that narrow plot, their own life's selfish bound.

V.

True, — in thy Childhood's Spring thou shalt not taste
The bitter toil of factory or mine:
Nor the Strong Summer of thy manhood waste
In labour vain, and want that bids thee pine:
The mellow Autumn of thy calm decline —
The sheltered Winter of thy happy Age —
Shall see home-faces still around thee shine —
No Workhouse threatening, where the heart's sick rage
Mopes like a prisoned bird within a cheerless cage.

VI.

True, that, instead of all this weary grief,
This cutting off what joy our life affords,
This endless pining for denied relief,
All Luxury shall hail thee! music's chords
Shall woo thee, — and sweet utterance of words
In Minstrel singing: Painting shall beguile
Thine eye with mimic battles, dark with swords, —
Green sylvan landscapes, — beauty's imaged smile, —
And books thy leisure hours from worldly cares shall wile.

VII.

There ends the sum of thy Life's holiday!
    WANT shall not enter near thee,—PLEASURE shall:
But Pomp hath wailed when Poverty looked gay,
    And SORROW claims an equal tax from all:
    Tears have been known from Royal eyes to fall
When harvest-trudging clowns went singing by:
    Sobs have woke echoes in the gilded hall:
And, by that pledge of thine Equality,
Men hail thee BROTHER still, though thou art set so high.

VIII.

DEATH, too, who heeds not poorer men's regret,
    Neither is subject to the will of Kings;
All Thrones, all Empires of the Earth are set
    Under the vaulted shadow of his wings:
    He blights our Summers, chills our fairest springs,
Nips the fresh bloom of some uncertain flower,
    Yea, where the fragile tendril closest clings,
There doth his gaunt hand pluck, with sudden power,
Leaving green burial-mounds, where stood Affection's bower.

IX.

Where is young Orleans? that fair Prince of France,
    Who 'scaped a thousand threatening destinies
Only to perish by a vulgar chance?
    Lost is the light of the most lovely eyes
    That ever imaged back the summer skies!
Widowed the hapless Wife, who seeks to train
    Childhood's frail thread of broken memories,
So that her Orphan may at least retain
The haunting shadow of a Father's face,—in vain!

X.

Oh! Summer flowers, which happy children cull,
    How were ye stained that year by bitter weeping,
When he, the stately and the beautiful,
    Wrapped in his dismal shroud lay coldly sleeping!
    The warm breeze through the rustling woods went creeping,

The birds with gladdening notes sang overhead:
  The peasant groups went laughing to their reaping,
But, in the gorgeous Palace, rose instead,
Sobs,—and lamenting Hymns,—and Masses for the Dead!

XI.

Where, too, is She, the loved and lately wived,
  The fair-haired Daughter of an Emperor,(49)
Born in the time of roses, and who lived
  A rose's life; one Spring, one Summer more,
  Dating from Girlhood's blushing days of yore,—
Fading in Autumn,—lost in Winter's gloom,—
  And with the opening year beheld no more?
She and her babe lie buried in the tomb,
The green bud on the stem,—both withered in the bloom!

XII.

Then, RUSSIA wept! Then, bowing to the dust
  That brow whereon proud Majesty and Grace
Are chiselled as in some ideal bust,—
  All vain appeared his power, his realm's wide space,
  And the high blood of his imperial race!
He sank,—a grieving man,—a helpless Sire,—
  Who could not call back to a pale sweet face
By might of rule, or Love's intense desire,
The light that quivering sank, in darkness to expire.

XII.

Where is the angel sent as Belgium's heir?
  Renewing hopes so linked with bitter fears,
When our own Charlotte perished young and fair,—
  The former love of long departed years!
  That little One is gone from earth's cold tears
To smile in Heaven's clear sunshine with the Blest,
  And in his stead another bud appears.
But when his gentle head was laid to rest,
Came there not boding dreams to sting his Father's breast?

XIV.

Of Claremont? of that dark December night,
    When, pale with weary vigils vainly kept, —
Crushed by the destiny that looked so bright, —
    Dark-browed and beautiful, he stood and wept
    By one who heard him not, but dumbly slept!
By one who loved him so, that evermore
    Her young heart with a fervent welcome leapt
To greet his presence! But those pangs are o'er,
And Heaven in mercy keeps more smiling days in store.

XV.

God hath built up a bridge 'twixt man and man,
    Which mortal strength can never overthrow;
Over the world it stretches its dark span, —
    The keystone of that mighty arch is WOE!
    Joy's rainbow glories visit earth, and go,
Melting away to Heaven's far-distant land;
    But Grief's foundations have been fixed below:
PLEASURE divides us: — the Divine command
Hath made of SORROW'S links a firm connecting band.

XVI.

In the clear morning, when I rose from sleep,
    And left my threshold for the fresh'ning breeze,
There I beheld a grieving woman weep;
    The shadow of a child was on her knees,
    The worn heir of her many miseries:
"Save him!" was written in her suppliant glance:
    But I was weaker than its fell disease,
And ere towards noon the Dial could advance
Death indeed saved her babe from Life's most desperate chance.

XVII.

The sunset of that day, — in splendid halls —
    Mourning a little child of Ducal race(50)
(How fair the picture Memory recalls!)
    I saw the sweetest and the palest face
    That ever wore the stamp of Beauty's grace,

Bowed like a white rose beat by storms and rain,
    And on her countenance my eyes could trace,
And on her soft cheek, marked with tearful stain,
That she had prayed through many a midnight watch in vain.

XVIII.

In both those different homes the babe was dead:
    Life's early morning closed in sudden night:
In both, the bitter tears were freely shed,
    Lips pressed on lids for ever closed from light,
    And prayers sobbed forth to God the Infinite.
From both, the little one was borne away
    And buried in the earth with solemn rite.
One, in a mound where no stone marked the clay,
One, in a vaulted tomb, with funeral array.

XIX.

It was the last distinction of their lot!
    The same dull earth received their mortal mould:
The same high consecration marked the spot
    A Christian burying-place, for young and old:
    The same clear stars shone out all calmly cold
When on those graves the sunset hour grew dim:
    And the same God in glory they behold, —
For Life's diverging roads all lead to Him
Who sits enthroned in light among the Cherubim!

XX.

None could revoke the weeping Beggar's loss, —
    None could restore that lovely Lady's child, —
Else untold sums had been accounted dross
    To buy, for one, the life that moved and smiled:
    Else had my heart, by false regret beguiled,
Recalled the other from his blest abode:
    One only power was left by Mercy mild,
Leave to give alms, — which gladly I bestowed
Where the lone tears had fall'n, half freezing while they flowed.

XXI.

Beautiful Royal Child, that art to me
  Only the sculptured image of a thought:
A type of this world's rank and luxury
  Through whom the Poet's lesson may be taught:
  The deeds which are by this world's mercy wrought,
Lie in the compass of a narrow bound;
  Our Life's ability,—which is as nought,—
Our Life's duration,—which is but a sound,—
And then an echo, heard still faintly lingering round!

XXII.

The sound being sweet, the echo follows it;
  And noble deeds should hallow noble names:
The very Ancestry that points a right
  To all the old hereditary claims,
  With a true moral worldly triumph tames.
What vanity Earth's riches to amass,—
  What folly to incur its thousand shames,—
When bubble generations rise and pass,
So swiftly, by the sand in Time's returning glass!

XXIII.

Pilgrims that journey for a certain time—
  Weak Birds of Passage crossing stormy seas
To reach a better and a brighter clime—
  We find our parallels and types in these!
  Meanwhile since Death, and Sorrow, and Disease,
Bid helpless hearts a barren pity feel;
  Why, to the POOR, should checked compassion freeze?
BROTHERS, be gentle to that ONE appeal,—
WANT is the only woe God gives you power to heal!

FINIS.

NOTES.

Note 1.

By stamping cold revenge an error of crazed wit.

The murder of Mr. Drummond, on the 20th of January, 1843, by D. Macnaughten, is probably still fresh in the memory of our readers: —

"After having been in attendance on Sir Robert Peel at the Privy Council Office, Mr. Drummond called at the bank to see his brother, and he left it again about four o'clock. As he was walking along close by the Salopian Coffee-house, a man was seen to present a pistol at him, and discharge it. He then drew another from his breast, but was seized by a policeman; and in the struggle the pistol went off while pointed downwards. Mr. Drummond, being wounded by the first discharge, staggered, and would have fallen, but was supported by a bystander, and with some difficulty he walked back to the bank. Mr. Jackson, an apothecary, was promptly in attendance on the wounded man; and he was without delay removed to his own house in Grosvenor Street, Grosvenor Square, where he died on the 25th. "

Macnaughten was tried for the murder: —

"The evidence for the prosecution occupied an entire day, and the case was adjourned. On the following day, Mr. Cockburn addressed the jury at great length, resting the defence upon the plea of insanity. He described the nature of the clear and positive evidence which he should adduce on this point; and proceeded to examine the law-authorities on the subject, —the opinion of Lord Hale, and the cases of Lord Ferrers, Hatfield, Bellingham, and others, contending that modern science had thrown so much light upon the organisation of the brain and its morbid condition, that the doctrine of the bench at earlier times must be received with caution. With regard to the case of Bellingham, who had been executed for the murder of Mr. Perceval, the general opinion now seemed to be, that the verdict in that case had been improperly obtained. Bellingham had been tried and executed only a week after the crime was committed; and it appeared that the application of his counsel to have the trial postponed had been refused, but that witnesses would have been ready to come forward, if the application had been granted, to make out decidedly the plea of insanity. In the case of Bowler, who had been subject to epileptic fits, and manifested all the indications of insanity, the prisoner was executed; and at the trial of Oxford, Baron Alderson remarked, 'Bowler was executed, I believe; and very barbarous it was. ' The Scotch authorities had taken a more humane view of the law. It was, for instance, the opinion of Mr. Baron Hume, that though a man might be in general conscious that murder was a crime, and yet commit a particular murder under the influence of some unaccountable delusion, he could not be held morally responsible for the crime. The true nature of the delusion which exempted from crime had been admirably laid down by Lord Erskine, who said, in his defence of Hatfield, that insanity might prevail upon a particular point, and that monomania exculpated an individual from the guilt of crime committed under its influence. Mr. Ray likewise held that a man might be as sane as the rest of the world on all points but one, and yet that an act committed under that particular delusion was one for which the man was no more answerable than if all his mental faculties had been deranged. "

Macnaughten was acquitted: —

"And, in consequence of the manner in which the trial terminated, and the strong expression of public feeling which it excited, it was determined by the House of Lords to refer certain questions to the judges on the state of the law relating to crimes committed by persons supposed to be insane or afflicted with monomania. " — Annual Register, 1843.

Note 2.

The mother's arms encircle him about.

In the autumn of 1843, I found two boys who had run away from home lying on some steps near a church; the younger was in such a state of exhaustion, that he could neither eat nor stand. After they had rested and slept at my house, I sent them home; and, as the elder boy seemed in great dread of the punishment which would be inflicted by his father, I wrote, advising that the wretched little wanderers (the least of whom was but six years of age) should receive a "free pardon" on their arrival. The father, a poor labouring man, heard my letter read in silence, held out his hand to the boy, and said that, in consequence of what had been written, he would not punish him. The mother, to use the language of the man to whose care I had entrusted them, "folded them up in her arms, over and over, and cried a good deal, before she spoke; then she said, 'Oh, my dears, I thought I'd seen the last of your two faces! '"

Note 3.

And ask, with all a heathen's discontent.

In Warburton's "Divine Legation of Moses" the following passage occurs:

"Religion establishing a providence, the rewarder of virtue and the punisher of vice, men naturally expect to find the constant and univocal marks of such an administration. But the history of mankind, nay, even of every one's own neighbourhood, would soon inform the most indiligent observer, that the affairs of men wear a face of great irregularity; the scene that ever and anon presents itself being of distressed virtue and prosperous wickedness; which unavoidably brings the embarrassed religionist to the necessity of giving up his belief, or finding out the solution of these untoward appearances. His first reflection might be with the poet Claudian: —

'Omnia rebar Consilio firmata Dei; qui lege moveri
Sidera, qui fruges diverso tempore nasci, —
Sed cum res hominum tanta caligine volvi
Adspicerem, lætosque diu florere nocentes,
Vexarique pios, rursus LABEFACTA CADEBAT RELIGIO. '

"But, on second thoughts, reason, that, from the admirable frame and harmony of the material universe, taught him that there must needs be a superintending providence to influence that order which all its parts preserve, for the sake of the whole, in their continued revolutions, would soon instruct him in the absurdity of supposing that the same care did not extend to man, a creature of a far nobler nature than the most considerable of inanimate beings. And therefore human affairs not being dispensed at present agreeably to that superintendence, he must conclude, that man shall exist after death, and be brought to a future reckoning in another life, where all accounts will be set even, and all the present obscurities and perplexities in the ways of providence unfolded and explained. From hence religion acquires resistless force and splendour; and rises on a solid and unshaken basis. "

Note 4.

So lives the little Trapper underground.

Lord Ashley's Bill has in a great measure done away with the horrors attendant on the employment of children in coal-mines. If there were not, still existing, employments almost as injurious and as melancholy in their effects, this passage might have been omitted; but the subject of the excessive labour performed by children in England, is one of which the details are so startling as to be scarcely credible. When Lord Ashley moved for leave to bring in his Bill, he briefly quoted the statements of the Report with respect to the ages of the children employed: —"'In South Staffordshire, Shropshire, Warwickshire, Leicestershire, and Cumberland, children begin to work at seven years of age; about Halifax, Bradford, and Leeds, at six; in Derbyshire and South Durham, at five or six; in Lancashire, at five; and near Oldham, as early as four; and, in some small collieries of the last neighbourhood, some children are brought to work in their bed-gowns. In North Durham and Northumberland, many children are employed at five or six, but not generally; that age is common in the east of Scotland; in the west of Scotland, eight; in South Wales, four is a very usual age; in South Gloucestershire, nine, or younger; in North Somersetshire, six or seven. In the south of Ireland, no children at all are employed. All the underground work, which in the coal-mines of England, Scotland, and Wales, is done by young children, appears in Ireland to be done by young persons between the ages of thirteen and eighteen. '

What the work of a "trapper" was, may be shewn in the following extracts from the Parliamentary Reports: —

"The air-door boy, or trapper, commonly the youngest person employed in the mine, has the charge of a door placed in a road, along which horses, men, and boys, are constantly passing, but through which it is essential to the ventilation of the mine to prevent the current of air from the downcast shaft from passing, in order that this current may be forced round the other roads and workings of the pit. The duty of the trapper is to open this door for persons who have occasion to pass through it, and then to shut it again as quickly as possible; and on his keeping this door constantly shut, excepting at the moment when persons are passing through it, the safety of the mine, and the lives of the persons employed in it, entirely depend.

"The trappers sit in a little hole scooped out for them in the side of the gates behind each door, where they sit with a string in their hands attached to the door, and pull it open the moment they hear the corves (i. e. carriages for conveying the coal) at hand, and the moment it has passed they let the door fall to, which it does of its own weight. If any thing impedes the shutting of the door they remove it; or, if unable to do so, run to the nearest man to get him to do it for them. They have nothing else to do; but, as their office must be performed from the repassing of the first to the passing of the last corve during the day, they are in the pit the whole time it is worked, frequently above twelve hours a-day. They sit, moreover, in the dark, often with a damp floor to stand on, and exposed necessarily to draughts. It is a most painful thing to contemplate the dull, dungeon-like life these little creatures are doomed to spend—a life, for the most part, passed in solitude, damp, and darkness. They are allowed no light; but sometimes a good-natured collier will bestow a little bit of candle on them as a treat. On one occasion, as I was passing a little trapper, he begged me for a little grease from my candle. I found that the poor child had scooped out a hole in a great stone, and, having obtained a wick, had manufactured a rude sort of lamp; and that he kept it going as well as he could by begging contributions of melted tallow from the candles of any Samaritan passers-by. To be in the dark, in fact, seemed to be the great grievance with all of them. Occasionally, they are so posted as to be near the shaft, where they can sometimes run and enliven themselves with a view of the corves going up with the coals; or, perhaps, occasionally with a bird's-eye peep at the daylight itself; their main amusement is that, however, of seeing the corves pass along the gates at their posts. When we consider the very trifling cost at which these little creatures might be supplied with a light, as is the case in the Cumberland collieries, there are few things which more strongly indicate the neglect of their comfort than the fact of their being kept in darkness—of all things the most wearisome to a young child.

"John Saville, seven years old, collier's boy at the soap-pit, Sheffield: 'I stand and open and shut the door; I'm generally in the dark, and sit me down against the door; I stop twelve hours in the pit; I never see daylight now, except on Sundays; I fell asleep one day, and a corve ran over my leg and made it smart; they'd squeeze me against the door if I fall to sleep again. ' Sarah Gooder, aged eight years: 'I'm a trapper in the Gauber Pit; I have to trap without a light, and I'm scared; I go at four and sometimes half-past three in the morning, and come out at five and half-past; I never go to sleep. Sometimes I sing when I've light, but not in the dark; I dare not sing then. I don't like being in the pit; I am very sleepy when I go sometimes in the morning. ' James Sanderson, eight years old: 'I am a trapper; I sit in the dark all the day, or I run to the bottom of the pit and come back. ' Samuel Hirst, aged nine years and four months, Jump Pit: 'I sit by myself; I never have a light; I sit still all day long, and never do any thing except open and shut the door. '

"William Martin, not ten years old, Messrs. Houldsworth's Colliery: 'I trap two doors; I never see the daylight except on Sundays. '"

There is something not only touching, but (to those who think seriously) awful and striking, in the fate thus simply told, and the struggle of the soul against it. The intelligence of the child who "manufactured a rude sort of lamp; " the quenchless gaiety of the other (a little girl), who "sometimes sang" when she had light! — what can poetry add to such descriptions?

Note 5.

Patient they lay, and longed for morning's blessed light.

This "want of light" is too often the fate of the poor under other circumstances. Not once, but in countless instances, I have been told by the poor of this; of the long dreary nights when they had to "wait" for light, in pain and anguish, being unable to afford even the rush taper, which would have been such a comfort. On one occasion a man told me he thought his wife had got better and gone to sleep, but in the morning, "when the light came, " he saw she had "gone to sleep for good. " I have remembered these instances in lighted ball-rooms, and connected them with a striking passage in St. François de Sale's "Introduction à la Vie Dévote: " —

"On fait les danses et les bals durant la nuit, et dans les ténèbres, qui ne peuvent être suffisamment éclairées par les illuminations;... tandis que vous dansiez, plusieurs personnes sont mortes dans une grande angoisse; mille milliers d'hommes et de femmes ont souffert les douleurs les plus violentes en leur maisons et dans les h'pitaux."

Note 6.

Might make him feel less weary and deject.

Of all the strange and mistaken attempts to regulate the morals and correct the vices of the lower classes, the measure proposed by Sir A. Agnew was surely the strangest, as well as the most oppressive and unjust, since its provisions could only have been carried into force against the Sabbath amusements of the poor, leaving the rich to act on their own discretion.

Note 7.

Come, creeping sadly to their hollow hearts.

A year or two has elapsed since the interference of the police and vigilance of inspectors forced on the public mind the painful fact, that after the driving, riding, and gay lounging of Hyde Park and Kensington Gardens were over for the day, those places of fashionable resort became, for the night, a sort of temporary "refuge for the destitute, " the houseless and homeless creeping into the trees and gravel-pits for shelter, and sleeping there. A gentleman, who signed himself "Anti-Humbug, " published a letter stating his belief that the parties who slept there were principally robbers and women of bad character, who not only were unworthy of compassion, but passed the night there by preference. His opinion did not become general, and the result of the fact becoming known was the establishment of several "refuges" in different parts of the metropolis, which afford shelter to those who see night coming on without having the means to secure a lodging. Many of those who have availed themselves of this temporary assistance have been persons of education and respectability, who had, indeed, seen "better days. "

Note 8.

Draws close her tatter'd shawl athwart her shivering breast.

> "Ah, turn thine eyes
> Where the poor, houseless, shiv'ring female lies:
> She once, perhaps, in village plenty blest,
> Has wept at tales of innocence distrest;

Her modest looks the cottage might adorn,
Sweet as the primrose peeps beneath the thorn;
Now lost to all, her friends, her virtue fled,
Near her betrayer's door she lays her head,
And, pinch'd with cold, and shrinking from the show'r,
With heavy heart deplores that luckless hour,
When, idly first, ambitious of the town,
She left her wheel and robes of country brown."

GOLDSMITH.

Note 9.

To see him thus attempt the sunny skies!

There is, in the possession of Mr. Rogers the poet, a picture by Guercino of unequalled beauty, representing a child watching a bird perched on the finger of his mother. The attitude of the child; his eager curiosity, mingled with a certain degree of fear; the leaning forward of his head while the little limbs are curling and shrinking away from the startling approach of the novel object of attention, are all life-like, and depicted with exquisite skill.

Note 10.

What flashing thoughts have woke to fade away?

Among the thousand instances of neglected genius, perhaps none is more curious than that exemplified in the life of Alexander Wilson, the celebrated writer on the birds of the United States.

"With an enthusiasm never excelled, this extraordinary man, who went to the United States a poor and unfriended Scotch weaver, first taught himself, at the age of forty years, to draw and colour after nature, then applied himself to the study of various branches of knowledge, and, having acquired the power of writing clearly and elegantly, as well as of depicting by his pencil what he saw in his rambles, set out to penetrate through the vast territory of the United States, undeterred by forests and swamps, for the sole purpose of painting and describing the native birds. During seven years, in which he prosecuted this undertaking, he travelled more than ten thousand miles, 'a solitary, exploring pilgrim, ' as he describes himself. His labours were rewarded with no worldly riches or honours, for he had the greatest difficulty in procuring subscribers for his splendid work, and, when a bookseller at last undertook to print and publish it, the only remuneration which the author received was a payment for the mechanical labour of colouring his own plates. But his soul was set upon the one object of his life—that of giving a complete account of one of the most interesting portions of the works of the Creator, as far as the vast continent of North America afforded him opportunities for diligent examination; and he passionately pursued his inquiry into the history of birds. "— RENNIE'S Bird Architecture.

Wilson's "American Ornithology" is now one of the most valuable works in a well-stored library.

Note 11.

The dull pollution of its stagnant air.

I can recollect seeing, when I was a child, one of the most celebrated beauties of the gipsy race—a woman of the name of Charlotte Stanley, whose portrait was painted by Sir Thomas Lawrence, and engravings made from it. Her hair, (which hung in long glossy ringlets of raven black,) she assured us she curled by twisting it round a hot tobacco-pipe. She said she could not sleep in a house; that she could not breathe freely; that she should die if she were obliged to give up her wandering life. In former days attempts had been made to induce her to do so, and an offer made to allow her a cottage rent-free; but the daughter of Ishmael continued a vagrant by preference. At the time I saw her she was still beautiful. She had a husband (who savagely ill-treated her, and was, I believe, hung for sheep-stealing) and several children.

Note 12.

I saw one man, armed simply with God's Word.

I had, accidentally, an opportunity of hearing Father Mathew during his stay in England, and have rarely been more impressed than by the scene I then witnessed. Having heard many arguments as to the amount of good likely to result from his efforts in behalf of temperance, I cannot help repeating here an observation I made at the time, —namely, that, without exception, all the persons I then saw, took the Temperance Vow apparently as a step towards a general reformation of previous evil courses, and not simply as a vow against drunkenness. All the persuasion exercised by those who wished relations or friends to take it, were based on this notion. As I stood in the crowd, I heard perpetually sentences that contained in themselves the pith of a hundred arguments. "Oh, take it, John, take it, and you'll not lose your work anymore! " "Take it, take it, and home 'ill be what it was! " "Take it, and, by the Lord's blessing, you'll not be tempted! " I saw a girl there, who told me she was twenty that day, and "had been drunk most nights since she was sixteen. " I never beheld a stronger expression of prayer in a human countenance, than when she knelt in the semicircular group surrounding the platform from which Father Mathew and others addressed the people. It was an affecting scene—affecting from the quiet simplicity and sincerity of the reverend father's eloquence, and from the earnest and often tearful attention with which his words were received. He has the advantage not only of a very clear and sweet voice, but of a style particularly suited to uneducated listeners, inasmuch as he indulges in none of the long, involved, oratorical sentences, which the poor, who never read, are unable to follow, or to comprehend. It was with very deep regret that I lately heard that Father Mathew had become involved in pecuniary difficulties, on account of his endeavours to pluck out by the roots, and by the aid of a religious vow, that vice which the poor themselves so frankly admit to be the cause of almost every error they commit. I saw a son—a hale, ruddy, honest-looking workman, persuade his father, and lift his cap off as he knelt down. I saw many women persuade their husbands; and, in one single instance, I saw a young woman try to persuade a sister or companion without effect. She tried very earnestly, and spoke very sensibly: the other, who was also young and very good-looking, answered scoffingly and in bad language. While they were dis- cussing the matter, the blessing was pronounced; the persuader sank on her knees (as did the persons immediately round), the girl she had addressed remained standing; and I can vividly recall her companion's look of sorrowful reproach, which seemed to imply that her standing was a sort of moral exile from those about her, and from the good work going on.

Note 13.

> And gloomy in the summer's smile
> Stands the "CHILD'S PRISON. "

For a detailed account of Parkhurst Prison, I would refer my readers to No. 449 and No. 601 of "Chambers's Edinburgh Journal, "—a paper containing more combined instruction and amusement than any other that I know, professing to be conducted on the same plan. I have abridged part of the account given there, and have added some particulars obtained from the kind-hearted and excellent Captain Woollcombe himself, when I visited the prison in the autumn of 1842. The correspondent of "Chambers's Journal" says: —

"The streets of no city in Holland, Belgium, Germany, and France, that I have seen, exhibit such a crew of dirty and miserable-looking little wretches as are to be seen daily in London, Edinburgh, Dublin, Glasgow, and other large seats of population, and whose almost homeless and lawless condition is a positive scandal to the community. Falling, as a matter of course, into the commission of petty delinquencies, they again and again figure before magistrates in the police-courts, and, improving as they proceed, by a vicious system of imprisonment, they in due time 'work their way, ' as it is called, to the bar of the Old Bailey, the Court of Justiciary, or some other of the higher tribunals.

"For a number of years back, it has not been customary to hang boys. The practice terminated with the reign of George III. Since that period, they have more usually been sent to the prison at Millbank, —to the Hulks in the Thames, where they have been compelled to work in a condition worse than that of brutes, —or transported to New South Wales, where they were assigned as slaves. In only a few instances, and these of a peculiarly favourable nature, have the convicts been reclaimed, instructed, or improved; the greater proportion having been turned loose on society, at home or abroad, much more deeply sunk in moral depravity than at the commencement of their course of servitude. Latterly, an immense improvement has been effected in the disposal of young male convicts. Instead of being permanently lodged in any penal establishments of the old stamp, they are, according to the judgment of the Secretary of State, sent to a prison or penitentiary in the Isle of Wight, " (now called Parkhurst Prison.)

"This establishment, which externally resembles a large suite of barracks for soldiers, inclosed with a lofty wall, is situated on the face of a rising piece of ground, about a mile and a half north from Newport, on the road to Cowes; and is, therefore, favourably placed, as respects both salubrity and convenience. There is also an advantage in its being placed on an island, as the chance of escape and connivance is by that means very materially lessened. For reasons which require no explanation, there is no indiscriminate admittance of strangers to see the interior; and it was only by an order from the Home Office, communicated to the governor, that I was enabled to make the visit which I desired.

"Captain Woollcombe, a gentleman who had for some years retired from active service, and engaged himself in benevolent plans of juvenile instruction on a private estate, had then the command of the institution, as governor and director. " (It is now in other hands.)

"The institution, as I learned, was first opened for the reception of inmates in December 1838, and, in the course of twelve months, the number sent to it was 157. At the time of my visit there were 180, and the accommodation will eventually admit 320. All the prisoners are boys from nine to sixteen years of age, the greater proportion, apparently, being from about eleven to thirteen, or of that age and appearance usually seen at day-schools. Each boy, on entering, is dressed in a coarse grey suit, with his number and the letters P. P. strongly marked on the breast. The objects sought to be attained by the course of treatment are twofold: —the penal correction of the boy, with a view to deter, not himself only, but juvenile offenders generally, from the commission of crime; and the moral reformation of the culprit.

"Captain Woollcombe's exertions, in the prosecution of this arduous and important work, have been ably supported by the Rev. Thomas England, who acts as chaplain.

Nearly one-half the number of boys were from London, and the remainder from the rest of England, with the exception of eleven from Scotland, one from the Isle of Man, and two from Quebec. Theft by house-breaking, and larceny, were generally the crimes for which they had been ultimately sentenced. Three were under sentence of fifteen years' transportation, one for fourteen years, fourteen for ten years, one hundred and fifteen for seven years, and one for five years; one for three years' imprisonment, thirteen for two years, one for eighteen months, two for twelve months, and two for six months. It is not proposed, I believe, to retain any of the prisoners beyond two or three years at Parkhurst, in which period, it is presumed, they will have been reclaimed from their evil propensities.

"The teaching of the boys some useful kind of trade, or labour, by which they may earn an honest subsistence on returning to society, is one of the most admirable arrangements connected with the institution. The trades now in regular course of teaching in the prison are those of tailors and shoemakers. Such painting and whitewashing as have been required have been done by the prisoners, as, also, some carpenters' work; but the latter occupation, as well as that of the smith's work, presents many temptations to criminal boys, in the use of tools for improper purposes, and, if carried to any extent, might cause much difficulty, by want of a regular supply of work. Tailoring and shoemaking are not open to these objections, and at these trades eighty-four boys are now (or were lately) employed for a few hours daily. The time allotted to out-door labour, either on the land attached to the prison or within the walls, as occasion may require, is about two hours every afternoon, except in wet weather, when the boys are employed in such work inside the prison as can be provided, such as cutting and tying wood for lighting fires, making mops from old junk for prison uses, &c.

"Being conducted into the work-rooms, I was shewn a pile of jackets and other articles of attire, and also a quantity of shoes, all which had been made by the boys, and seemed of good workmanship. Captain Woollcombe expected shortly to be able to undertake a contract for clothing for the army. "

This was in 1840. In 1843, the same journal again resumes the subject:—

"The report presented to parliament of the condition of this prison during the year 1842 is highly gratifying. Since its formation in 1838, the system adopted for reforming and instructing, rather than punishing, juvenile culprits, has been steadily and most successfully carried out. The number of prisoners during the past year was 375, of ages varying from between eight and ten, to between eighteen and twenty-one years. They were divided into two classes, according to their aptitude for learning and practising various trades; and although, at the formation of the establishment, it was found inexpedient to intrust the prisoners with the dangerous tools of the carpenter, &c., this restriction no longer exists; and during the past year classes of carpenters, sawyers, coopers, and bricklayers, have been formed under superintending tradesmen of each class, in addition to the tailors and shoemakers at work from the first. The proficiency attained by these classes has been satisfactory, and, in some cases, beyond expectation. The young sawyers have cut up 37,636 superficial feet of timber, felled from the prison lands. The elder and strongest boys only can be employed as sawyers; their proficiency in work is reported to be good, many of them being able to measure and line the timber preparatory to cutting it.

"Circumstances have prevented more than ten prisoners being instructed in the cooper's art; and although they only commenced work in July last, they made, by December, 483 articles well enough to be received into her majesty's stores, for the use of the public service.

"The twelvemonth's work of the tailors produced 6242 garments; the shoemakers made 2206 pairs of shoes, and thirty-one leather caps. The greatest portion of the clothes and shoes have been applied to the convict service; some for home consumption at Parkhurst, and the rest for boys embarked from the prison for the colonies. Besides handicraft, agricultural labour is carried on by the Parkhurst prisoners, upon a farm belonging to the establishment. Good quantities of oats, hay, potatoes, &c., were produced in spite of a dry season, and other disadvantages; and four acres of recently reclaimed land were cropped with turnips, oats, and potatoes. The stock on this miniature farm is small, but quite adequate to teaching the prisoners various matters of management connected with cattle and other live stock.

"As regards improvement, of 119 admitted in 1838, 108 have, up to this time conducted themselves well, and are in a very hopeful state.

"Of 116 prisoners admitted in 1840, the report is equally favourable. By the table of the state of the schools on the 31st December, 1842, we find that, out of 240 prisoners, the conduct of 116 of them had been good, 104 indifferent, but only twenty decidedly bad.

"The chief difficulty which the authorities feel, is to know what to do with the discharged prisoners when thoroughly reformed. By a wise regulation, the government have pardoned several deserving prisoners, upon the condition that they emigrate to one of our free colonies, providing them with a suitable outfit. Of the prisoners removed during the past year, 110 have been discharged under such pardon. They quitted the prison in a very becoming state of mind, truly grateful for the boon granted to them. Two have been pardoned unconditionally, and restored to their friends, their health being unequal to the active labour required in the colonies. The short sentences of two others having expired, they were also discharged. Sixteen have been transported as incorrigible, as provided by the regulations of the prison; and three have been removed by authority of the Home-Office, as unfit for colonial life: they were deficient in moral and mental power, and diseased in body. Only two deaths have occurred from the commencement of the establishment, and they took place last year. "

In proof of the ignorance in which these little criminals are often found, we have the Government Report of 1844, which states that, —

"Since the opening of that prison, 596 persons, whose ages vary from eleven to twenty, have been admitted; and the following statistics exhibit their comparative attainments:

	Capacity of Reading.	Capacity of Writing.
Well	21	7
Tolerably	131	110
Imperfectly	233	172
Scarcely at all	95	66
Not at all	116	241
	596	596

"It thus appears that only 21 out of the 596 were able to read well, and only 7 to write well. Scarcely any of them had any knowledge of Scripture, the meaning of words, or general information; and upwards of 100 were altogether without instruction. "

In proof of the natural intelligence of these neglected creatures, and of their capacity for instruction, Captain Woollcombe told me many interesting anecdotes. They had, at first, been allowed to correspond at intervals with their relatives; and the permission to write was looked upon as a sort of reward for steady conduct. The practice, however, of sending these letters was discontinued, the accounts of the prison given by the young convicts being so favourable that they seemed to be better off than those who had committed no crime. The letters, though not sent, were occasionally written; nor were the young prisoners aware that they never would reach the parties for whom they were intended. Some few of them I read; and one, in particular, addressed by the boy to his mother, affected me to tears; so full was it of protestations of amendment, of exultation at having learned a trade, and of assurances that he would support her in her old age, when his imprisonment should be over. The letter was not to go; the boy was not to return. The termination of his imprisonment was to be exile from his native country, —a just, a necessary exile; but that did not make his letter the less touching. I may here state, on Captain Woollcombe's authority, that the mothers of these boys almost always wrote them letters of advice and consolation; the fathers seldom, in comparison; but many of the children had been driven to crime by the neglect and cruelty of step-mothers. I asked if they were very unhappy; and was assured that the great mass were not the least so, but that, on the other hand, there was no doubt that a few were heart-broken. The ties of home, in many instances, retain their influence. One apparently hardened little fellow, who swore and played the bully on coming into the prison, nevertheless sank down in tears on being talked to of "his little sister. " This boy retained sufficient merriment and ingenuity, in his state of punishment, to contrive a caricature of the man who superintended the tailors' board and taught the boys tailors' work, by cutting a figure of a man riding a donkey, out of the cloth of two contrasted colours used for the prison dresses. I saw this figure, in which the eyes were worked with black and white thread, and which was very neatly executed. This signal act of audacity was discovered in consequence of a general laugh from his little fellow-convicts. Governor Woollcombe took much pains with this boy; he was intelligent, improved rapidly, reformed, and went to the colonies under favourable circumstances. Besides this memorable donkey-and-rider, of prison-cloth, I was shewn various rude carvings, similar to those used for umbrella and cane handles, scraped and carved with pocket-knives, out of the bones left at the boy's dinner on "meat days. " As I stood in that court-yard full of juvenile felons, I asked whether they manifested in truth more corrupted dispositions than usual. Captain Woollcombe then said he did not think there were more bad boys than in any other large school, and that he regretted that the establishment was called a PRISON, that originally it was called the Reformatory, and that he was sorry the name had been altered. I cannot better conclude this note than by presenting to the reader a poem copied verbatim as composed by one of these young convicts. In itself, it is a poor and prosaic ballad, in doggerel verse; but the circumstances of its authorship may give it the same interest in the eyes of others, which it had for me. The lad whose death it laments, was a fellow-prisoner, who was returned when dying of consumption, to his friends: —

"CHARLES REYNOLDS.

I.

"All you who young and healthy are
    Attend to what I say,
And think not that 't will always be
    With you as 'tis to-day.

II.

The young do not always escape
    Affliction's chastening rod;
For they, as oft as aged folks,
    Are called to meet their God.

III.

You who are young and healthy now,
    May, ere this year be flown,
Be pale and weak, or you may be
    In prime of life cut down.

IV.

One of our comrades, who was once
    A stout and healthy lad,
Has been cut down in prime of life,
    And numbered with the dead.

V.

He was among the first who were
    Confined within this wall,
And he's the first whom it has pleased
    Almighty God to call.

VI.

Charles Reynolds was a healthy lad
　　When we at first came here,
And perfect health he did enjoy
　　For upwards of a year.

VII.

But very soon it pleased the Lord
　　To take his health away,
And he who strong and healthy was,
　　Now weak and helpless lay.

VIII.

In pain and sorrow, day and night,
　　He on a sick-bed lay,
And lingered till his stout-made form
　　Was wasted much away.

IX.

And then it pleased the Lord to take
　　His chast'ening hand away,
And He who loved him did again
　　To him fresh strength convey.

X.

When he got well he was again
　　Welcomed among our throng;
But sickness seized him yet again,
　　And laid him up ere long.

XI.

It pleased the Lord yet once again
　　Disease on him to pour,
And he, the once stout, healthy lad,
　　Join'd in our sports no more.

XII.

When he had suffered here some time,
    His pardon down did come,
His mind was eased when he was told
    That he was going home.

XII.

He to his home was then convey'd
    To see his parents dear,
And there he thought upon the things
    That he had been taught here.

XIV.

He pray'd that God for Jesus' sake
    Would give him a release
From all his pain; God heard his prayer—
    He died in perfect peace.

XV.

A Christian lady, kind and good,
    A letter here did send,
To let our Governor know the state
    Of poor Charles Reynolds' end.

XVI.

'T was joy to hear that Reynolds was
    Relieved from all his pain,
But more to hear that he was not
    Instructed here in vain.

XVII.

May all, O Lord, who shall come here,
    Believe Thy Holy Word;
And humbly hope to die like him,
    Through Jesus Christ our Lord!"

This poem is printed from the copy given to me by Captain Woollcombe, without correction or erasure; and was composed by one of the condemned boys in the prison at Parkhurst, Isle of Wight.

Note 14.

E'en as in solitude its light had risen!

The one blot in the plan of this excellent institution, was the occasional infliction of solitary confinement; a punishment dreadful at any age, and as dangerous as inhuman when acting on a young mind. A very melancholy case occurred at Parkhurst, in which the boy's untoward violence amounted almost to madness, and he pulled down portions of the plastering on the wall of his cell. This boy was afterwards insane, and died in the hospital there. I cannot state at what interval from his confinement this took place. I saw the two instances I have noticed in my poem: they were not allowed to go into school, but Captain Woollcombe and the chaplain visited them.

Note 15.

He might not now stand there, condemned for crime.

Wilkes, with a light irony ill suited to so grave a subject, observed, "The worst use you can put a man to, is to hang him. " The Lord Chief Justice Hale, in a spirit of more decent gravity, remarked, that "A sound, prudent method for an industrious education of the poor, will give a better remedy against their corruptions than all the gibbets and whipping-posts in the kingdom. " It was Hale, also, who prophesied that the want of such an education, and of "a due provision for relief in a way of industry, " would fill the gaols with malefactors, and the kingdom with idle persons, increasing, even to a desolation, in time!

Note 16.

Till some fair form, with smiles and blushes bright.

On the occasion of the launch of the TRAFALGAR, Her Most Gracious Majesty performed the "christening rite, " and broke the bottle on the bows of the vessel.

Note 17.

To rouse our Heroes, and our armèd Powers.

See the glorious passage in a speech made by Mr. Canning, on being presented with the freedom of the town of Plymouth: —

"Our present repose is no more a proof of inability to act, than the state of inertness and inactivity in which I have seen those mighty masses that float in the waters above your town, is a proof they are devoid of strength, and incapable of being fitted out for action. You well know, gentlemen, how soon one of those stupendous masses, now reposing on their shadows in perfect stillness—how soon, upon any call of patriotism, or of necessity, it would assume the likeness of an animated thing, instinct with life and motion—how soon it would ruffle, as it were, its swelling plumage—how quickly it would put forth all its beauty and its bravery, collect its scattered elements of strength, and awaken its dormant thunder. Such as is one of these magnificent machines when springing from inaction into a display of its might—such is England herself, while apparently passive and motionless she silently concentrates the power to be put forth on an adequate occasion. But God forbid that occasion should arise! "

Note 18.

And hunger-pangs the DEATH-LOT shall appease.

The horrible fact here alluded to, is familiar to those who have read many narratives of shipwrecks; one of the most fearful accounts is that of the sufferings of the crew who escaped on a raft from the wreck of the French frigate Méduse, lost off the coast of Africa. I have no opportunity of referring to that account, nor to the statement of similar events in the American ship Peggy, where the men drew lots which of them should perish, that his body might become food for the survivors. The man who drew the lot calmly requested the surgeon to bleed him to death, which was done; those who fed on his flesh were taken ill; but it is doubtful (from a comparison with other instances) whether the revolting meal was the real cause of their illness. The following is abridged from Cyrus Redding's "Shipwrecks and Disasters at Sea, " and is part of the narrative there given of the sufferings of six men who deserted from the garrison at St. Helena in June 1799, with the intention of joining an American brig, which they failed to reach: —

"Provisions running very short, they restrained themselves to an ounce of bread in twenty-four hours, and two mouthfuls of water.

"They continued on the same allowance until the 26th, when all their provisions were consumed. On the 27th, M'Quin took a piece of bamboo in his mouth to chew, and all the rest followed his example. It being Brown's turn that night to steer the boat, he cut a piece from one of his shoes, recollecting to have read of people in a similar situation eating their shoes. But he was obliged to spit it out, as it was soaked with salt water; therefore he took the inside sole, part of which he ate, and distributed some to the others, but it gave them no relief.

On the 1st of July, Parr caught a dolphin with a gaff, that had been left in the boat, on which they all fell on their knees, and thanked God for His goodness to them. They tore up the fish, and hung it out to dry. On this they subsisted until the 4th, when, finding the whole expended, bones and all, Parr, Brown, Brighouse, and Conway, proposed to scuttle the boat, and let her go down, that they might be put out of their misery. The other two objected, observing, that God, who had made man, always found him something to eat.

"M'Kinnon, about eleven o'clock on the 5th, said, he thought it would be better to cast lots for one of them to die, in order to save the rest, to which they consented. The lots were made; but Parr having been sick two days with the spotted fever, was excluded. It was his province to write the numbers out, and put them into a hat, from which the others, blindfolded, drew them, and put them in their pockets.

"Parr then asked whose lot it was to die: none knew what number was in his pocket, but each prayed to God that it might fall on him. It was agreed that he who had number five should die; and the lots being unfolded, M'Kinnon's was number five.

"They had previously agreed, that he on whom the lot fell should bleed himself to death, for which purpose they had provided themselves with nails from the boat, which they sharpened. M'Kinnon with one of them cut himself in three places, in the foot, hand, and wrist, and, praying God to forgive him, died in about a quarter of an hour.

Before he was quite cold, Brighouse cut a piece of flesh off his thigh with one of the same nails, and hung it up, leaving his body in the boat. About three hours after they all ate of it, but only a very small bit, and the piece lasted until the 7th of the month. Every two hours they dipped the body in the sea in order to preserve it.

"Parr, having found a piece of slate in the bottom of the boat, sharpened it on the mooring-stone, and cut out another piece of M'Kinnon's thigh with it, which lasted them until the 8th. It was then Brown's Watch, and he, observing the water change colour about break of day, called the rest, thinking they were near the shore, but, as it was not quite daylight, they saw no land. As soon as day appeared, however, they discovered land right a-head, and steered for it, and were close in with the shore about eight in the morning.

"There being a heavy surf they endeavoured to turn the boat's head to it, which, from weakness, they were unable to accomplish, and soon afterwards the boat upset. Brown, Parr, and Conway, got on shore, but M'Quin and Brighouse were drowned.

"On the prisoners informing the people that they were English, they were immediately released, and three hammocks provided for them, in which they were carried to the governor, who allowed them to lie in his own bed, and gave them milk and rice to eat, but they were seized with a locked-jaw, from not having ate any thing for a considerable time, and continued ill until the 23d. "

Note 19.

As his for whom Griefs wild and piercing cry.

The son of Admiral Sir R. Otway was lost in the sloop Victor, which vessel he commanded. The Victor sailed from Vera Cruz (where the men had been suffering from fever) to Halifax, on the 31st August, 1842, and was never heard of afterwards. This afflicting bereavement was preceded by the sudden death of another son, in the prime of youth, who was thrown while riding in Hyde Park, and died of the injuries received in the fall.

Note 20.

Yet thou hast wept, —like him whose race is run.

The fate of the good and gallant son of Admiral Sir John Gore cannot be more touchingly narrated than in the brief and simple letter addressed by his bereaved father to the Admiralty, giving official information of the event. I subjoin the letter entire: —

"Melville, off Cape L'Aguillas, "5th May, 1835.

"SIR, —It has become my painful duty to request you to state to the Lords Commissioners of the Admiralty the death of Lieutenant James Lewis Fitzgerald and Lieutenant John Gore (flag lieutenant), together with eight seamen (as per margin), belonging to H. M.S. ship bearing my flag, the circumstances of which are as follows: —

"On the 30th of April, being about thirty-eight leagues to the eastward of Algoa Bay, the weather towards sunset confirmed the appearance during the day of approaching storm, and rendered it necessary to reef the courses, &c. &c., in doing which Henry Phillips fell from the fore-yard overboard. Lieutenant Gore saw he could not swim (and having had the happiness of saving a man's life, and confident of his powers, hoping to do so again), he leaped overboard while the boats were lowering. Two cutters were sent as expeditiously as possible, Lieutenant Fitzgerald in one, Lieutenant Hammond in the other; their search was decreed to be fruitless, though continued until dark. Lieutenant Hammond's boat returned safe, Lieutenant Fitzgerald's was within hail of the ship, when a heavy squall and one of those hollow destructive seas, so peculiar to this latitude, broke directly into her, and neither the boat nor any thing belonging to her was picked up. It was then impenetrably dark, and the gale continued until next day at noon.

I have the honour to be, sir,

"Your most obedient humble servant, "JOHN GORE, Vice-Admiral."

The Fairy, surveying vessel, was never heard of after she left Harwich, on the 12th of November, 1840; her crew and officers perished with her. Among the latter was lost a most promising youth, son of Sir C. Adam, who had but lately joined the ship.

The loss of the steamer President, with the long anxiety and terror endured by the relatives and friends of those on board, is still fresh in the memory of the public.

Note 21.

Which the betraying breeze hath backward blown.

In deer-stalking, so keen is the sense of these animals, that it is found impossible to approach near enough to fire upon them, unless the wind be directly contrary. A wounded deer always, if possible, takes to the water.

Note 22.

Peruvia's Incas, when, through lands unknown.

The Incas of Peruvia are described by all the authorities who have written on the history and conquest of Mexico, as a most beautiful and majestic race, slender and stately in appearance, or what is sometimes termed "high-bred" looking. They were active and manly, but proved quite unequal to the tasks of drudgery in the mines, imposed on them by the cruel and tyrannical Spaniards, and perished in great numbers. Of their endurance and bravery of spirit many interesting anecdotes are told, besides the story familiar to most readers, of the Inca, who being, with his minister, Guatimozin, bound on red-hot bars, and hearing the latter complain with groans of the torture, said gently, "Am I, then, on a bed of roses? "

Note 23.

Ben-Doran glows like iron in the forge.

Ben-Doran is one of the most beautiful of the mountains in Perthshire. The glow and the fading of the sunset on the Highland hills literally answers to the above simile. The most evanescent of all things is a gleam of light; yet, I believe there are few persons who do not retain vividly in their minds a fixed and lasting impression of one or more of these "effects, " as they are called. For my own part, I have a long imaginary gallery of these "transient pictures, " taken by land and sea, wherever I found them, as faithfully, though not as visibly, as by the Daguerrotype process. There, I and my good companion Memory, walk up and down on dim grey winter days, and refresh ourselves with contemplation; and there the ghost of youth is apt to join us, and induce us especially to pause over "Highland Mornings" (where the white soft clouds are melting and lifting from the emerging hills) and "Highland Evenings" (where the

sunset light lies on the earth like the halo round a saint's head.)
Since the passage to which this note refers was written, one other
reality has become only a remembrance, in consequence of the death
of the kind-hearted companion and friend of those Highland days,
my brother-in-law, Sir Neil Menzies, whose habitation, when I was
with him, was chiefly by

"That lone lake's unforgotten blue, " Loch Rannoch, in Perthshire.

Note 24.

> And mock with howling fury at the porch
> The ever-listening God, in his own holy church.

The unfortunate disputes which have arisen during the last few
years in the Scotch church were, in 1843, productive of scenes of
violence, which all must have regretted, however strenuously and
conscientiously either party may have desired to uphold their
opinions. After the secession of the "Free Church" party, they carried
on, with much vigour and energy, the work which they had
commenced. " They sent their emissaries through the empire,
collecting subscriptions, extending their numbers and connexions,
and courting the sympathy and alliance of other ecclesiastical
communions with whom they were able to identify themselves by
any common bond. Their efforts in building churches, however,
were thwarted in several quarters by the refusal of the landholders
to allow them sites for the purpose. Several proprietors, among
whom were some noblemen of great influence, thought proper to
decline being parties to the propagation of what they probably
deemed an unjustifiable and dangerous schism by affording any
facilities to the Free Church. This opposition created much
indignation and bitterness among that party. In the course of the
autumn of this year, some serious disturbances took place in Ross-
shire, and elsewhere, in connexion with the Free Church movement.
The people alleging the refusal of the landowners to grant sites in
justification of their outbreak, took the law into their own hands, and
attempted forcibly to resist the induction of sonme of the new
ministers substituted for the seceders. Churches were barricaded,
and the obnoxious presentees driven away and assailed with stones
and other personal violence. At the settlement of a new minister at
the parish of Resolis, in Cromarty, so formidable a mob assembled,
taking possession of the church, and making demonstrations of
extreme violence, that a body of the coast-guard were sent for, the

Riot Act was read, and at last it became necessary to fire upon the mob. Fortunately, no injury was done by the discharge, but to avoid the necessity of endangering the lives of the people by a further using of fire-arms, the civil authorities thought it prudent to retire, and the new minister was inducted in the inn. The next day a violent mob invaded the town of Cromarty, broke open the gaol, and rescued one of the persons captured in the preceding affray. Some serious hurts were received by those who resisted the rioters. " — Annual Register.

Note 25.

Yea! rather fear "the image of a voice. "

This expression occurs in a beautiful passage in 2 Esdras, chap. v. ver. 37.

Note 26.

The Lamb's calm City wrapt in one Eternal Dawn.

"And the city had no need of the sun, neither of the moon to shine in it: for the glory of God did lighten it, and the Lamb is the light thereof. "And the gates of it shall not be shut at all by day, for there shall be no night there. " — Revelation, chap. xxi. ver. 23-25.

Note 27.

And bathed in bloody sweat on dark Gethsemane's night.

For this stanza I am indebted to the kindness of a friend (far better able to treat such a subject), to whom I submitted the passage when the proofs were in course of correction, and who modelled the rough-cast of my thought into a different shape.

The following passage is to be found in Cave's "History of the Apostles: "

"And here we may justly reflect upon the wise and admirable methods of the Divine Providence, which in planting and propagating the Christian religion in the world, made choice of such mean and unlikely instruments, that he should hide these things from the wise and prudent, and reveal them unto babes; men that had not been educated in the Academy, and the schools of learning, but brought up to a trade, to catch fish and mend nets; most of the Apostles being taken from the meanest trades, and all of them (St. Paul excepted) unfurnished of all arts of learning, and the advantages of liberal and ingenuous education: and yet these were the men that were designed to run down the world, and to overturn the learning of the prudent. Certainly had human wisdom been to manage the business, it would have taken quite other measures, and chosen out the profoundest rabbins, the acutest philosophers, the smoothest orators, such as would have been most likely by strength of reason and arts of rhetoric to have triumphed over the minds of men, to grapple with the stubbornness of the Jews, and baffle the finer notions and speculations of the Greeks. We find that those sects of philosophy that gained most credit in the heathen world did it this way, by their eminency in some arts and sciences, whereby they recommended themselves to the acceptance of the wiser and more ingenious part of mankind. Julian the Apostate thinks it a reasonable exception against the Jewish prophets, that they were incompetent messengers and interpreters of the Divine will, because they had not their minds cleared and purged, by passing through the circle of polite arts and learning. Why, now this is the wonder of it, that the first preachers of the gospel should be such rude, unlearned men, and yet so suddenly, so powerfully prevail over the learned world, and conquer so many, who had the greatest parts and abilities, and the strongest prejudices against it, to the simplicity of the gospel. When Celsus objected that the Apostles were but a company of mean and illiterate persons, sorry mariners and fishermen, Origen quickly returns upon him with this answer, 'That hence 'twas plainly evident, that they taught Christianity by a Divine power, when such persons were able with such an uncontrolled success to subdue men to the obedience of his word; for that they had no eloquent tongues, no subtile or discursive head, none of the refined and rhetorical arts of Greece to conquer the minds of men. '

'For my part, ' says he, in another place, 'I verily believe that the Holy Jesus purposely made use of such preachers of his doctrine, that there might be no suspicion that they came instructed with arts of sophistry, but that it might be clearly manifest to all the world, that there was no crafty design in it, and that they had a Divine power going along with them, which was more efficacious than the greatest volubility of expression, or ornaments of speech, or the artifices which were used in the Grecian compositions. '''

Note 28.

Whose message to the earth was Peace and Love.

A startling and curious example of the effect produced on what we are pleased to term "savage minds, " by the discrepancy between the profession of a religion of peace and the alleged necessity of warfare, is given by the present Bishop of New Zealand, in an account (not published) of his progress through that country. I have received permission to extract the passage from the Bishop's private journal.

"August 23, 24, 25, 26. —Examined candidates for confirmation and baptism. Found the minds of the natives very much unsettled by the late war. Many held very conscientious scruples about renewing the public profession of Christianity and coming to the Lord's Table, when they were liable at any moment to be called out to war. They quoted the words of the 37th Article, as translated in the Maori Prayer-book, 'that it is lawful for Christian men, at the command of the magistrate, to wear weapons, and serve in the wars; ' and, of course, felt it to be inconsistent with the state of peace described and required in the Gospel. Many stayed away in consequence. "

Note 29.

Retracing with sunk heart his morning track.

The immense distances which the poor have to go, before it can be decided whether they are to be relieved or not, is one of those flaws in the plan of the New Poor-law which so obviously require re-consideration and reform. In an inquest lately held on the death of a labouring man, named William Murrell, it was proved that his wife journeyed twenty miles before she obtained an order for grocery, &c. in relief, worth three shillings! I have made an extract from one of my brother's letters to shew what the law and the practice is in the Dorchester Union; and it is the same in others: —

"The law and the practice is, that if a pauper residing in a Union requires relief, he or she, be they able-bodied or otherwise, must first make their application to the relieving officer: if their distress be urgent, he is empowered to relieve them imemediately, and report the circumstance to the Board of Guardians on the ensuing board-day. If the relieving officer should be of opinion that the pauper is not actually starving, he directs him to present himself at the Union

House at the next weekly meeting of the Board of Guardians. Now, observe the excessive hardship of this. The relieving officer of the Dorchester Union lives in my village. His district extends nearly in a circle of seven miles. A pauper, therefore, living at this distance from his house is compelled first to come to the relieving officer to make known that he is out of work and requires relief for himself and family. The relieving officer asks a few questions, does not consider it an urgent case, solely because the man had probably been employed until within a few days of his application, and tells him to attend at the Union House the following Wednesday, when the Board of Guardians will take the case into consideration. This probably might take place on Friday when he has walked fourteen miles there and back to see the relieving officer. He then has to wait Saturday, Sunday, Monday, and Tuesday, without employment, and probably without any other food but the potatoes from his garden. He is afraid to run in debt at the baker's, perhaps they are disinclined to give him credit. Wednesday comes, and he has to travel twelve miles to the Union House. I am not exaggerating the distance. When there, he is called before the Board, composed generally of farmers; possibly the chairman may be a man of property, and there may be a magistrate (who is an ex-officio guardian) present. The pauper's case is then read from "the Application and Report Book" of the relieving officer.

"William Soper, aged 31, his wife Ann, 33, with five children, their ages 9, 8, 4, 2, 1. He is able-bodied, 'out of work, and requires relief. ' He is then asked various questions by different guardians, as to where he was last employed, and by whom, the receipt of wages at the time, and whether he had had any piece-work, &c.

"In a case like this, (which is an every-day case,) the pauper is told, 'We cannot relieve you out of the house, we will direct the relieving officer to make out an order for the house; ' and thus it is entered in the book. The poor fellow then walks back twelve miles (in Soper's case it was nine, which made eighteen in the course of the day), to tell his family that he can have no relief except in the house. They linger on for a few days longer in the hope of obtaining employment, still feeding on potatoes for breakfast, dinner, and supper; and, then a large rate-payer in the parish may probably offer him a job, at 7s. per week, sooner than he shall go into the house, which he knows will cost the parish 2s. 6d. per head, which would be 17s. 6d. per week. The job lasts ten days, perhaps a fortnight, and then a fresh application to the relieving officer; the same long weary walk to his house and back, with the same reply; the same long weary walks to the Union House on the Wednesday following, and the same heart-breaking result. This time he goes into the Union House, where he is separated from his wife, and employed in cracking bones with a long iron pestle (which blisters his hands) in a kind of wooden mortar. This is out-door work. Last Wednesday, two lads were brought before the Board for fighting in the Union House. They had quarrelled because one had thrown into the other's mortar portions of bone which were difficult to crush. "

In the case of W. Murrell there was an inquest, from the newspaper report of which the following passage is given. The wife herself had been ill, and they had struggled on, half-starved, endeavouring to avoid the necessity of going into the workhouse:—

"Last Tuesday week deceased became very poorly, and, at the persuasion of the wife, consented that she should apply for medical relief. She accordingly on that morning left Ruislip Common, between seven and eight o'clock, and walked to Hillingdon, to the residence of Mr. Stockwell, the relieving officer for the Uxbridge Union, where she arrived about nine o'clock. He gave her an order on Mr. Rayner, surgeon, at Uxbridge, to whose house she proceeded with it, and then returned home to Ruislip Common, which she reached about twelve o'clock, having in the interim walked ten miles in a very weak state, and without (having no money) bringing any food or sustenance for her sick husband. Soon after her return home, Mr. Rayner visited them, and, immediately on ascertaining their destitute condition, he gave them an order for necessaries, which he desired the wife to take to Mr. Stockwell. The poor jaded wife then retraced her steps to Hillingdon, where the order of Mr. Rayner was exchanged by Mr. Stockwell for an order on Mr. Collins, a tradesman in Rnislip village, for grocery, &c., to the value of 3s., with which supply she reached her home in the evening, having in obtaining it had to traverse no less than twenty miles of ground. On the following Friday, she went to the Board of Guardians at the Uxbridge Union Workhouse, at Hilingdon, to ask for more relief, and told them that her husband had got a promise of work on the following Monday, and Mr. Peirce, one of the guardians, having stated that he had directed his bailiff to set the deceased at work in grubbing, the board ordered her to have her dinner, and Mr. Stockwell came out and told her to meet him at Ruislip Church on the next day (Saturday). On her doing so, he gave her three loaves and 1s. 8d½. in money, being equivalent to another 3s. On that day (Saturday) the deceased was very poorly, and on the Sunday he complained that he had knocked his foot against a stump, and, as the night advanced, getting worse, the wife called in the witness Hill, who found the deceased lying on the bed, a chaff one, on his face, when he complained of pain in his neck, and his jaw being locked. He was, however, quite sensible, and could speak to the last of his life. Mrs. Allday, the third witness, on the Tuesday morning went to Uxbridge to fetch Mr. Rayner, but the deceased died before he could arrive. Mrs. Allday stated that her husband had no employment but breaking stones at the Uxbridge Union Workhouse, at which he could never earn more than 1s. 4d. or 1s. 6d. a-day, and to perform that work he had to walk ten miles a-day.

"Mr. William Rayner, surgeon, of Uxbridge. — The immediate cause of death was pressure on the brain and spinal marrow. Both the vessels of the brain and the spinal marrow were turgid to a degree. Witness had never before seen such a case in his life. Could not state that want of food would produce lock-jaw. Considered that the state of the toe was more likely to produce lock-jaw.

"The coroner then said he trusted that the inquiry would produce good results. It was a melancholy and deplorable thing for the poor to have to travel twenty miles before they could obtain 3s. worth of relief. It was making their lives a life of toil and trouble, instead of affording them relief.

"The room was then cleared of strangers, and, on the public being again admitted, the jury returned a verdict of 'Died from lock-jaw; ' and

"The foreman said, that the jury could not separate without expressing their great dissatisfaction and disgust at the continuance of a system which compelled the poor, in the hour of sickness and destitution, to travel so many miles as it was proved that the wife of the deceased man was compelled to walk, before she could obtain the relief that was necessary for their wants. "

Note 30.

His "harbour and his ultimate repose. "

> "I would be at the worst; WORST is my port,
> My harbour, and my ultimate repose I"

—MILTON.

Note 31.

The self-denying hearts that shared the scanty store.

The generosity of the poor to each other fairly puts the rich to blush. There is scarcely an inquest held, in which it does not appear that the lingering starvation endured was relieved and delayed by the alms bestowed by those who could least afford to spare it. And the same generosity holds good in the bestowal of what to them is "income, " namely, their time. In cases of sickness, or helpless and bedridden confinement, it is astonishing how much time is bestowed as charity, —the truest and best charity. In cases even of removal from one poor cottage to another, I have heard the labouring class offer "a day" and "half a day" of the time on which their earnings depended, to assist in transporting the furniture and effects of a neighbour, suffering and helpless.

Note 32.

Received none, struggled on, and died of want's excess.

In one instance, which circumstances impressed very deeply on my mind, a pauper narrated to me his gradual fall to beggary, not as a means of exciting compassion, but as a defence, for allowing his children to become street mendicants: "I was hurt, " he said, "falling from a ladder where I was at work as a bricklayer. I broke my leg, I broke my arm, and I was ruptured; if any one had helped me then, things would have come round: no one helped me. I pawned every thing; the mother sent the eldest child out to beg, —that brought in something; we sent the others. And, now, if they don't beg, what is to become of us? If I'd been helped at the right time, I don't think it would ever have come to this. "

Note 33.

And baffled Famine seized his long-resisting prey.

Many of my readers probably saw (and, if they saw, are not likely to forget) the report last winter of a case of suicide by a poor sempstress, named Mary Alloways: —

"On the table was a letter, which had been written by the wretched woman just before her death. It produced many tears amongst the jurymen and spectators. The following is a copy of the letter: —

"'Mrs. White, 41 Castle Street, Oxford Street. "'Dear Friend, —I have spent many anxious hours and sleepless nights. I cannot obtain work; therefore it is impossible I can pay my rent, and I have preserved my watch as the only means that I have to put me in the ground. I have had it valued 10l. I judge that it will not cost more than 5l. to lay me in the grave in a humble way. The life I now live is a miserable one, and has been for several years. I have no one to care for me. Heaven is merciful! Yet a little while, and this feverish and unquiet spirit, I most sincerely hope, will be at rest with the hope that the Almighty will pardon me. Was I sure of that, I should leave the world without the least regret. I must chance what many great people have done before me. I am obliged to all friends that have been kind to me. My dear friend, I hope you will let some one follow me to the grave, but that I leave to you. I do not wish any one here to know my affairs. You will do as you please with my clothes. I am sorry to say that I owe Mrs. White this day seven weeks' rent (Nov. 5). I am very sorry to leave the world in debt. If my clothes and watch will not pay the expenses of my funeral and rent, it is my wish to be sent to the workhouse. My watch you will find in the large trunk. Adieu! God bless you all! My pen is so bad I fear you will not make out what I have written, and my mind is agitated. '

"The poor creature lodged in the back attic of the house. She had made no complaint of illness on the day that she was last seen alive, and the extent of her distress was not known in the house. Mrs. Jones, the witness, said deceased was an extremely well-behaved woman, and had been highly educated. They always imagined she had some trifling income that helped to support her, but since her death they had found such was not the case, but that she supported herself by the needle. She had lately appeared very desponding, which she stated arose from inability to procure work, and the poor wages she received. She had once or twice adverted lately to the double suicide at Kilmarnock, and said she would rather follow that example than apply for relief. She had some friends who occasionally gave her food; but she seldom had any other meals but breakfast and tea. Mr. Foxstaff, on examining the stomach, and the dregs of the cup alluded to, found that both contained oxalic acid, of which poison she had died. The deceased had all the appearance of having been completely starved. The jury returned a verdict, 'That the deceased destroyed herself by taking oxalic acid; but that there was no evidence of the state of her mind. '"

The first case that made the public aware of the extraordinarily small sums paid to poor needle-women, was that of the Miss Reynolds, daughters of Major Reynolds, who were making shirts at three half-pence a-piece. This case, which occurred at the Whitechapel office (Hon. G.C. Norton), was largely subscribed to. A Society for the relief of distressed Needlewomen now exists; and a long list of fashionable names follows that of Lord Ashley, as head of the association. The fact of the excessive hours of over-work, and the small remuneration accorded, is no novelty; but the combination of a section of the rich to prevent this one cause of misery, is a novelty, and one worthy of notice.

What may be done to save and rescue, in hours of terrible temptation and despair, was illustrated by another case at the Whitechapel office. The captain of a merchant-ship, who was brought before Mr. Norton for attempting to commit suicide, after a long struggle with adverse fortune, was relieved from the poor's box; and some encouraging advice was given him by the magistrate. Three or four years afterwards he returned with the amount, and stated, that he had begun again as a sailor before the mast, and had again become master. He said the magistrate had "put a new heart in him. "

Note 34.

Too often, like the stone-closed Arab well.

The wells in Arabia and Syria are often covered up with a flat stone, for the purpose of keeping out the sand, or to prevent cattle from doing them any harm. Jacob's well was so covered when Rachel approached.

"Then Jacob went on his journey, and came into the land of the people of the east. And he looked, and behold a well in the field, and, lo, there were three flocks of sheep lying by it; for out of that well they watered the flocks: and a great stone was upon the well's mouth. And thither were all the flocks gathered: and they rolled the stone from the well's mouth, and watered the sheep, and put the stone again upon the well's mouth in his place. And he said, Lo, it is yet high day, neither is it time that the cattle should be gathered together: water ye the sheep, and go and feed them. And they said, We cannot, until all the flocks be gathered together, and till they roll the stone from the well's mouth; then we water the sheep. And while he yet spake with them, Rachel came with her father's sheep: for she kept them. And it came to pass, when Jacob saw Rachel the daughter of Laban his mother's brother, and the sheep of Laban his mother's brother, that Jacob went near, and rolled the stone from the well's mouth, and watered the flock of Laban his mother's brother. " — Genesis, chap. xxix. ver. 1, 2, 3, 7, 8, 9, 10.

Note 35.

Who doth "pervert the judgment" of the poor.

"Cursed is he that maketh the blind to go out of his way. Cursed is he that perverteth the judgment of the stranger, the fatherless, and the widow. " — Commination: Book of Common Prayer.

Note 36.

NEUTRALITY, the cursed of Heaven.

"I know thy works, that thou art neither cold nor hot: I would thou wert cold or hot! " — Revelations, chap. iii. ver. 15.

Note 37.

Well spoke the Poet-Heart so tried by woe.

A Scotch weaver — Thoms, the poet of Inverary — recently describing the state of mind which, in his own person, destitution and the sight of his starving family engendered, eloquently says: —

"I felt myself, as it were, shut out from mankind — enclosed — prisoned in misery — no outlook — none! My miserable wife and little ones, who alone cared for me—what would I not have done for their sakes at that hour! Here let me speak out—and be heard too, while I tell it—that the world does not at all times know how unsafely it sits—when Despair has loosed Honour's last hold upon the heart—when transcendent wretchedness lays weeping Reason in the dust—WHEN EVERY UNSYMPATHISING ONLOOKER IS DEEMED AN ENEMY—who THEN can limit the consequences? For my own part, I confess that, ever since that dreadful night, I can never hear of an extraordinary criminal, without the wish to pierce through the mere judicial view of his career, under which, I am persuaded, there would often be found to exist an unseen impulse—a chain, with one end fixed in Nature's holiest ground, that drew him on to his destiny. "

Note 38.

And he must grieve down sorrow.

I do not know if this expression, beautiful in the original German, will appear forced and unnatural in English. It occurs in Schiller's tragedy of the "Death of Wallenstein" in the lament over the young and gallant-hearted Max Piccolomini: —

> "Verschmerzen werd' ich diesen Schlag, das weiss ich,
> Denn was verschmerzte nicht der Mensch? "

I have seen it variously rendered: —

> I know I shall forget this blow, at last;
> What will not man forget?
> From things most dear
> Even as from things most common is he weaned
> By the omnipotence of circumstance. "

Where the "forget" spoils all.

In the earlier editions of Coleridge's works, the lines are given: —

> "This anguish will be wearied down, I know.
> What pang is permanent with man? "

In Pickering's edition of 1835, the passage stands corrected: —

147

"I shall grieve down this blow, of that I'm conscious.
What does not man grieve down? "

And this translation is approved and commented upon in the preface to A. Hayward's celebrated translation of Faust; a translation said to be so faithful, that, were it possible for the original to be lost, Goëthe's poem might be re-written from this English version.

However inadequately given, the passage in "Wallenstein" must always strike the reader, not only on account of its marvellous beauty and eloquence, but for the simple truth of its description of that struggle with grief which all have felt; when Reason opposes to the strong present heart-ache, the prophecy founded on experience, that like all else on earth it will "pass away. "

Note 39.

Like Ormonde's Ossory, in his early doom.

The noted speech of the Duke of Ormonde: "I would not change my dead Ossory for any living son in England. "

Note 40.

Rose in a language foreign to their foes.

In De Foe's novel of the "Cavalier, " an anecdote is told of one who had served his country bravely, and was in all respects a gallant soldier; but, fighting in the Civil Wars, and slaying his opponent, he was suddenly smit with horror as though he had been a murderer, hearing the cry for quarter addressed to him in his native tongue.

Note 41.

And scenes that chill the soul, though vital strength surtives.

The horrors of the retreat of the British in the Affghan War are told with graphic detail in Lady Sale's journal: —

"December 24, 1841. —I received a note from Lawrence, enclosing one from Conolly (Sir William's nephew) to Lady Macnaghten, and had the sad office imposed on me of informing both her and Mrs.

Trevor of their husbands' assassination: over such scenes I draw a veil. It was a most painful meeting to us all.

"The Affghans still tell us we are doomed, and warn us to be particularly cautious of our safety in going out of cantonments. Taj Mahommed says that Mrs. Sturt and I must wear neemchees over our habits—common leather ones—and turbans, and ride mixed in with the suwars; not to go in palkees or keep near the other ladies, as they are very likely to be attacked.

"It was the general's original intention to halt at Begramee; but the whole country being a swamp encrusted with ice, we went on about a mile farther, and halted at about 4 P. M. All scraped away the snow as best they might, to make a place to lie down on. The evening and night were intensely cold: no food for man or beast procurable, except a few handfuls of bhoosa, for which we paid from five to ten rupees.

"Previous to leaving cantonments, as we must abandon most of our property, Sturt was anxious to save a few of his most valuable books, and to try the experiment of sending them to a friend in the city. Whilst he selected these, I found, amongst the ones thrown aside, Campbell's Poems, which opened at Hohenlinden; and, strange to say, one verse actually haunted me day and night: —

> Few, few shall part where many meet,
> The snow shall be their winding-sheet;
> And every turf beneath their feet
> Shall be a soldier's sepulchre.

' I am far from a believer in presentiments; but this verse is never absent from my thoughts. Heaven forbid that our fears should be realised!

"January 8. —At sunrise, no order had been issued for the march, and the confusion was fearful. The force was perfectly disorganised, nearly every man paralysed with cold, so as to be scarcely able to hold his musket, or move. Many frozen corpses lay on the ground. The Sipahees burnt their caps, accoutrements, and clothes, to keep themselves warm.

"The ladies were mostly travelling in kajavas, and were mixed up with the baggage and column in the pass: here they were heavily fired on; many camels were killed. On one camel were, in one kajava, Mrs. Boyd, and her youngest boy Hugh; and in the other Mrs. Mainwaring, and her infant, scarcely three months old; and Mrs. Anderson's eldest child. This camel was shot. Mrs. Boyd got a horse to ride; and her child was put on another behind a man, who being shortly after unfortunately killed, the child was carried off by the Affghans. Mrs. Mainwaring, less fortunate, took her own baby in her arms. Mary Anderson was carried off in the confusion. Meeting with a pony laden with treasure, Mrs. M. endeavoured to mount, and sit on the boxes; but they upset; and in the hurry pony and treasure were left behind; and the unfortunate lady pursued her way on foot, until after a time an Affghan asked her if she was wounded, and told her to mount behind him. This apparently kind offer she declined, being fearful of treachery; alleging as an excuse that she could not sit behind him on account of the difficulty of holding her child when so mounted. This man shortly after snatched her shawl off her shoulders, and left her to her fate. Mrs. M.'s sufferings were very great; and she deserves much credit for having preserved her child through these dreadful scenes. She not only had to walk a considerable distance with her child in her arms through the deep snow, but had also to pick her way over the bodies of the dead, dying, and wounded, both men and cattle, and constantly to cross the streams of water, wet up to the knees; pushed and shoved about by men and animals, the enemy keeping up a sharp fire, and several persons being killed close to her. She, however, got safe to camp with her child.

"Poor Sturt was laid on the side of a bank, with his wife and myself beside him. It began snowing heavily. Johnson and Bygrave got some xummuls (coarse blankets) thrown over us. Dr. Bryce, H.A., came and examined Sturt's wound: he dressed it: but I saw by the expression of his countenance that there was no hope. He afterwards kindly cut the ball out of my wrist, and dressed both my wounds.

"11. —We marched; being necessitated to leave all the servants that could not walk, the Sirdar promising that they should be fed. It would be impossible for me to describe the feelings with which we pursued our way through the dreadful scenes that awaited us. The road covered with awfully mangled bodies, all naked: fifty-eight Europeans were counted in the Tunghee and dip of the Nullah; the natives innumerable. Numbers of camp-followers, still alive, frost-bitten and starving; some perfectly out of their senses, and idiotic. Major Ewart, 54th, and Major Scott, 44th, were recognised as we passed them, with some others. The sight was dreadful; the smell of the blood sickening; and the corpses lay so thick, it was impossible to look from them, as it required care to guide my horse so as not to tread upon the bodies. But it is unnecessary to dwell on such a distressing and revolting subject.

"On the return of the troops after their set-out in the morning, commanding officers had great difficulty in collecting sixty files a corps; but even of these many could scarcely hold a musket; many died of cold and misery that night. To add to their wretchedness, many were nearly, and some wholly, afflicted with snow-blindness.

"They descended a long steep descent to the bed of the Téezeen Nullah. At this dip the scene was horrible: the ground was covered with dead and dying, amongst whom were several officers; they had been suddenly attacked, and overpowered. The enemy here crowded from the tops of the hills in all directions down the bed of the Nullah, through which the route lay for three miles; and our men continued their progress through an incessant fire from the heights on both sides, until their arrival in the Tézeen valley, at about half-past four P. M.

"The descent from the Huft Kohtul was about 2000 feet; and here they lost the snow.

"About 12,000 persons have perished!

"At the commencement of the defile, and for some considerable distance, we passed 200 or 300 of our miserable Hindostanees, who had escaped up the unfrequented road from the massacre of the 12th. They were all naked, and more or less frost-bitten; wounded, and starving, they had set fire to the bushes and grass, and huddled all together to impart warmth to each other. Subsequently, we heard that scarcely any of these poor wretches escaped from the defile; and that, driven to the extreme of hunger, they had sustained life by feeding on their dead comrades.

"14. —Shumshudeen Khan refuses to give up the Ghuznee prisoners. Only Lumsden and his wife are killed. Col. Palmer is said to have died of a fever; but whether brought on by the torture said to have been inflicted on him, or not, is not known.

"Four of our regiments are at Gundamuk, erecting a fort.

"Mrs. Trevor gave birth to another girl, to add to the list of captives."

Lieutenant Eyre gives similar descriptions: —

"A cruel scene took place after this, in the expulsion from the fort of all the unfortunate Hindoostanees, whose feet had been crippled by the frost. The limbs of many of these poor wretches had completely withered, and had become as black as a coal; the feet of others had dropped off from the ankle; and all were suffering such excruciating torture as it is seldom the lot of man to witness. Yet the unmerciful Giljyes, regardless of their sufferings, dragged them forth along the rough ground, to perish miserably in the fields, without food or shelter, or the consolations of human sympathy.

"We retraced our former track down the bed of the stream, and across the hills, to the fort where General Elphinstone died. A few miles descent made a great difference in the climate and the progress of vegetation; the wild roses were every where in full bloom, and, with other gay flowers, scented the air and enlivened the scene. We crossed a branch of the Tezeen valley; a short cut over the hills led us to the foot of the Huft Kotul, or hill of seven ascents. Here we once more encountered the putrid bodies of our soldiery, which thenceforward strewed the road as far as Khoord Cabul, poisoning the whole atmosphere. A littl beyond Kubbur-i-jubbar we passed two caves, on opposite sides of the road, full as they could hold of rotten carcasses. Thence to Tungee Tureekee the sight became worse and worse.

"May 24. —Again on the move at 9 A. M. The Khoord Cabul pass being now absolutely impassable from the stench of dead bodies, we took the direct road towards Cabul. "

Well may he at length exclaim: —

"That we should have escaped unhurt, with so many delicate women, young children, and tender infants, through such numerous perils, fatigues, and privations; and, above all, from the hands of such merciless enemies as Akbar Khau and his Giljye confederates, seemed at first too much for the senses to realise! "

Note 42.

In thy first "prime of life" — victorious Wellington!

At a dinner given by the East India Directors on Sir H. Hardinge's departure from England, the Duke of Wellington, in returning thanks, observed: — "But we have not met here to-day to talk of bygone transactions, though I am very grateful for the mention of services I had the honour of rendering to the East India Company, — when I was in India, — IN THE PRIME OF MY LIFE. " The casual expression of the Veteran Hero struck those who heard and saw him, and was responded to by a burst of cheering.

It is a curious fact that a letter is said to be extant, containing an application from Mr. Arthur Wellesley (then a very young officer), for a small place at the disposal of government, as "he wished to leave the army, and marry. " The future hero was fortunately unsuccessful on that one occasion, and lived to be "Duke of Victory. " The following is taken from the list of peers in the House of Lords: —

"Arthur Wellesley, Duke, Marquis, Earl, and Viscount Wellington, Marquis Douro, Field Marshal, a Cabinet Minister, Commander-in-Chief, Warden of the Cinque Ports, Colonel of the Grenadier Guards, Colonel-in-Chief of the Rifle Brigade, Constable of the Tower of London, Chancellor of the University of Oxford, Lord Lieutenant and Custos Rotulorum of Hampshire and of the Tower Hamlets, Governor of Plymouth, Master of the Trinity House, Governor of the Charter House, Field Marshal of Austria, Russia, Prussia, and the Netherlands, K.G. G.C. B., Grand Cross of the Royal Hanoverian Guelphic Order, Knight of the Golden Fleece, ot San Fernando of Spain, of Grand Cross of Maria Theresa of Austria, of St. George of Russia, Black Eagle of Prussia, Tower and Sword of Portugal, Elephant of Denmark, Sword of Sweden, William of the Netherlands, Annunciade of Masimilian Sardinia, Joseph of Bavaria, and many others: also Duke of Ciudad Rodrigo, a Grandee of the first Class, and Captain General in Spain, Duke of Vittoria, Marquess of Torres Vedras, and Conde de Vimiera, and Marshal General in Portugal, Prince of Waterloo in the Netherlands, " &c.

Note 43.

Hath something in it of the old command.

The great Field-Marshal's style, when speaking in debate, is curt, dry, frank, and somewhat imperious. On a celebrated occasion, he concluded the observations he had made, with a grave but familiar warning: "Well, my lords, I have told you; so, take care! " His friends and admirers feel while listening to him, that he is speaking that which he knows to be the truth; his foes and opponents admit that he is speaking that which he believes to be the truth. The least eloquent of all the principal debaters in the House of Lords, his speeches are nevertheless listened to with the profoundest attention, and carry a weight with them not always the result of the most masterly efforts of rhetoric.

Note 44.

In Bethlehem's rocky shrine, he can but mark, —

The "Shrine of Bethlehem" was one of the subjects at the Diorama some time ago, and was given with a wonderful effect of reality. A description of it may be found in "Eöthen: " —

"The village of Bethlehem lies prettily couched on the slope of a hill. The sanctuary is a subterranean grotto, and is committed to the joint guardianship of the Romans, Greeks, and Armenians, who vie with each other in adorning it. Beneath an altar gorgeously decorated, and lit with everlasting fires, there stands the low slab of stone which marks the holy site of the Nativity; and near to this is a hollow scooped out of the living rock. Here the infant Jesus was laid. Near the spot of the Nativity is the rock against which the Blessed Virgin was leaning, when she presented her babe to the adoring shepherds.

"Many of those Protestants who are accustomed to despise tradition consider that this sanctuary is altogether unscriptural—that a grotto is not a stable, and that mangers are made of wood. It is perfectly true, however, that the many grottoes, and caves which are found among the rocks of Judea, were formerly used for the reception of cattle; they are so used at this day; I have myself seen grottoes appropriated to this purpose. "

An account is also given in Mr. Warburton's interesting volumes, "The Crescent and the Cross: " —

"Entering by a very low door and long passage, almost upon hands and knees, I stood up under the noble dome of the Church of St. Helena. The roof, constructed of cedar-wood from Lebanon, is supported by forty huge marble pillars, shewing dimly the faded images of painted saints. The whole building is silent, dirty, and neglected-looking, but of noble proportions.

"The chapel of the Nativity is a subterranean grotto, into which you descend in darkness, that gives way to the softened light of many silver lamps suspended from the roof. Notwithstanding, the improbability of this being the actual place of the Nativity, one cannot descend with indifference into the enclosure, which has led so many millions of pilgrims in rags or armour during 1800 years from their distant homes: It is, however, impossible to recognise any thing like a reality in the mass of marble, brass, and silken tawdry ornaments; and one leaves this most celebrated spot in the world with feelings of disappointment. "

Note 45.

To what good actions that small book gave birth.

"The Christmas Carol, " by C. Dickens, Esq., will stand its ground as one of the best of sermons on charity, however little the style of its pages may resemble a solemn discourse on the relative duties of rich and poor.

Note 46.

> Eke out the measure of thy fault, and sin
> "First with her, then against her, " —

See "Philip Van Artevelde, " Act V. Scene I., —a work which a most competent judge pronounced to be the finest dramatic poem of modern days: —

> .... "But, call my weakness what you will, the time
> Is past for reparation. Now to cast off
> The partner of my sin, were further sin,
> 'T were with her first to sin, and next against her. "

Note 47.

And "sleep came with the dew, " and gladness with the dawn.

This line, with a slight alteration of metre, I have taken from a beautiful collection of "Rural Poems, " by Mr. William Barnes of Dorchester. A collection shut in a great measure from the public by that which makes Burns's Poems a sealed book to many readers; namely, the peasant-dialect in which it is written. The volume by Mr. Barnes opens with a very curious dissertation on the Dorset dialect, and is in all respects well worthy of attention. The following is the passage quoted from: —

> "When we, in chilehood, us'd to vind
> Delight among the gilcup flow'rs,
> Al droo the zummer's zunny hours;
> An' sleep did come wi' the dew! "

Note 48.

And the Bad Angel stained the heart of man.

For a curious fable on original sin, see page 65 in Milnes' "Palm Leaves, " where two angels come to the nurse who held Mohammed in her arms: —

"One, with a mother's gentleness, then took the slumbering child
That breathed as in a happy dream, and delicately smiled:

Passed a gold knife across its breast, that opened without pain,
Took out its little beating heart—all pure but one black stain.

Amid the ruddy founts of life in foul stagnation lay
That thick black stain like cancerous ill that eats the flesh away.

The other form then placed the heart on his white open hand,
And poured on it a magic flood, no evil could withstand:

And by degrees the deep disease beneath the wondrous care
Vanished, and that one mortal heart became entirely pure.

With earnest care they laid it back within the infant's breast,
Closed up the gaping wound, and gave the blessing of the blest:

Imprinting each a burning kiss upon its even brow,
And placed it in the nurse's arms, and passed she knew not how.

Thus was Mohammed's fresh-born heart made clean from
Adam's sin,
Thus in the Prophet's life did God his work of grace begin. "

Note 49.

> The fair-haired daughter of an Emperor
> Born in the time of roses.

"The Grand-Duchess Alexandra, fourth daughter of the Emperor of
Russia, and consort of his Royal Highness Prince Frederick of Hesse,
eldest son of the Landgrave William of Hesse. The imperial family
were prepared for the sad termination of the Grand-Duchess's
illness, which, it is well known, was the principal cause of the
emperor's hasty departure from this country. The young princess, so
prematurely cut off, was born 24th of June, 1825, and was married
September 1843 to the Prince Frederick of Hesse. "

Note 50.

Mourning a little child of Ducal race.

The extent of poetical license here taken consists in having
compressed two days into one. I did actually witness the death of a
poor infant in circumstances of most painful destitution, the day
before I saw the same loss mourned by one who dwells in a palace,
built I believe for the Duke of York when heir apparent to the
English crown; and truly I then saw

> "The sweetest and the palest face
> That ever wore the stamp of beauty's grace! "

I had written some lines previously, on the death of the "little child
of ducal race; " and I have often since felt grateful to the gift of
poetry, which earned for me, without intention, a friendship I trust I
shall never lose, —a friendship whose root was in the gentle
thoughts that spring from an innocent grave!

Note 51.

WANT is the only woe God gives you power to heal.

There is no point so hotly disputed as the degree of aid (if any), and what sort of aid, should be afforded to the poor; more especially to the pauper poor, those who sink to begging alms. I am tempted to reprint portions of letters written by me, some years since, on a narrow section of this great question, namely, metropolitan alms-giving. To those who have so little sympathy as to attribute merely to vanity the owning and reprinting of these observations, I have nothing to say, except that I wrote them without the name, which like Romeo's, seems "no part of me, " and for the sake of their subject: though I will frankly own, that I am not sorry to prove, as I close the pages of this book, that I have not suddenly broke out into rhyming on what is now become a leading topic in men's mouths; but have, as far as my ability and position permitted, constantly supported opinions which some whom I respect and esteem consider unsound; but which others, as wise, as good, and more merciful, hold to be just and true. The letters were published in January 1841: —

ALMS-GIVING IN THE METROPOLIS.

To the Editor of the Times.

SIR, —The many columns devoted to the cause of the poor in your admirable paper embolden me to hope that space will be afforded to some observations on the abuse of private charity recently alluded to in the case of Margaret Walsh, namely, aims-giving in the metropolis, or, as your writer terms it, 'thoughtless alms-giving. '

"The late Mr. Walker (author of the Original, and for many years magistrate for the district of Whitechapel) held an opinion, founded on his own personal observation and experience among the poor, that no man, however humble his trade or occupation, ever came to such distress as to be reduced to solicit alms, unless through drunkenness, improvidence, rash and dishonest speculation, or want of common industry—in short, that excess of poverty was invariably a man's own fault. Following out this principle, Mr. Walker disapproved of all alms-giving, as tending to weaken the self-dependence of the labouring classes, by the dangerous example of the relief so afforded. He had written a pamphlet, embodying most of the severe provisions of the present New Poor Law, nearly twenty years before that measure came into operation; and, though a kind-hearted and generous man, I cannot recollect a single case of the many we discussed together, in which he thought it just or fit that 'charity' should be given. Relief by alms was in his eyes a premium on improvidence, a reward for sin and folly.

"The opinions of Mr. Walker are those of a large and daily increasing class. I think the fault of those opinions, the fault of the New Poor Law, and the fault of the reasoning which is becoming the fashion—for there is a fashion even in this—consists in the painful fact, that whereas we used to hold ourselves bound to relieve our starving fellow-creatures, we now hold ourselves bound to sit in judgment on them. We are grown such theorists as to the causes of their distress, that the distress itself is scarcely heeded; and the varieties of disease, privation, and suffering, which come under our notice, are no longer treated as if they involved life and death, flesh and blood, but as mere available examples of pro and con arguments. We are accused of having formerly encouraged the vices of the poor by too indulgent a consideration of their necessities. God knows, we have now well-nigh forgotten their necessities in too stern a consideration of their vices.

"The present result of these new rules and axioms is, (I am informed by clergymen and others well calculated to give an opinion,) a great addition to the sums distributed in private charity, and an increased disposition to 'thoughtless alms-giving. ' The thinkers of the day having decided that relief ought not to be afforded, it is on the 'thoughtless aims-givers' that the poor chiefly rely. But the poor know, as well as we do, how little real charity or principle there is in these alms; they know, that whereas the thinkers deny their claim, the thoughtless forget it, and it is melancholy to observe how sharp-witted misery will make them; how the 'simple cunning' peculiar to the childish, the helpless, and the uneducated, enables them to make an intuitive calculation of the quickest methods to rouse compassion; and how the latent consciousness that it has been an effort of their own skill, rather than a spontaneous movement of heart-pity, destroys all gratitude when they have succeeded.

"The poor feel they are not thought of; and there is no trick of cunning they will not adopt to force attention. They will borrow on loan each other's pawn-tickets, hospital-admissions, and certificates of distress, and pay a consideration out of what is thus obtained.

They will hire each other's children at so much per day; they will affect lameness, blindness, fits, &c. We are content with blaming the imposture without seeking into its cause. The neglect of the rich is the bad rank soil, from which springs the hypocrisy of the poor!

"The thinker reproves the thoughtless alms-giver for giving to common street-beggars. He saw with his own eyes the woman he relieved go into the next public-house. She bought gin, instead of a loaf for her young family, horrid drunken creature! And the old couple, whose blankets were taken out of pawn, have pawned them again, and sold the counterpane provided; and the man who pretended to have seven children has only four—three have been dead these six years; and the consumptive woman who could not nurse her baby turns out not to be its mother at all, but to have had it left with her, being deserted by its own 'unnatural' parent, and now she makes her market of the infant by this cunning device. All, in short, is perfidy, imposition, and ingratitude; and the thoughtless alms-giver acknowledges her folly, and remarks in self-excuse, that it was so painful to see them stand shivering at the carriage window, but that she 'really will leave off giving to London beggars. '

"That evening, perhaps, the thinker and the thoughtless alms-giver are at a fashionable party. They hear the news of the day discussed. An improvident love-match has been made against parental consent; an accomplished man of fashion has destroyed himself; General So-and-so's nephew is dead at the age of twenty-eight, from hard drinking. Now, mark how they sympathise with that young couple; how they lament, without blaming, the rashly departed; —'Poor fellow! with all his expectations, to go off in this way! What a pity no one could induce him to break through the habit of drinking! And Captain L., too, —after his debts had been paid three different times, to gamble away his last farthing, and shoot himself at last! It is very melancholy—very sad, indeed! '

"It is very melancholy; but there is something sadder yet to think upon, and that is, the different measure with which we have meted out, and continue to mete out, our sympathy to the rich and to the poor. The rich man's nephew has perished young, because he could not resist the vice of drinking. The rich man's son has shot himself, because he could not forbear the sin of gambling. We think upon them as we knew them—smiling, social, gay—and groan for very pity when we reflect on the distress of surviving relatives. Where is the shivering woman who crept away with her baby, and spent a few pence in gin? Where is the reckless and improvident labourer, reduced through his own fault to ask alms? Where are the uneducated victims of the vices that were too strong for these educated men? There is no reply. We feel for, we comprehend the temptations of pleasure, but who takes thought for the temptations of pain?

"When the rich shall acknowledge their superfluity to be held as a trust to be distributed, the poor will acknowledge it a trust to be employed; it is the want of accompanying sympathy and consideration that causes 'thoughtless alms-giving' to be both mischievous and useless. No sacrifice is made on the one part, and no obligation is felt on the other; the alms given and received create not a moment's fellowship between the giver and receiver. The real root of the evil lies, not in the bestowing of alms, but in the want of proper feeling for those on whom alms are bestowed.

"The proof of this may be found in the fact of the immense disproportion of benefit conferred by those who assist the poor in the country, and those who give casual alms in towns. Do not let us be content with superficial and false reasoning on this point. It is easy to say, in the country there are no 'gin-palaces, ' no crammed and suffocating fever districts, no idle, dissolute, and unemployed crowds hustling each other for a mouthful of bread, no streets swarming with alternate examples of the most profuse luxury and the most bitter want; the root of the matter lies not in these things. They may be discouragements, but they can never be preventives to the exercise of a sound charity. Do not tell us that it is impossible adequately and effectually to relieve the objects who claim our compassion in the paved thoroughfares or intricate by-ways of London; the street-beggar is not of a different race from his fellow-poor, nor is there any thing, either in his nature or situation, to render vain the assistance which it is admitted would enable the labouring villager successfully to struggle through the hour of misfortune. No, there is much to render difficult and to impede the efforts of those who would fain not be 'thoughtless alms-givers, ' but nothing that can neutralise those efforts and make them of no avail. There is no irremediable evil in this world, except sin, and the evil we are now discussing lies in a very narrow compass, and admits of a very easy remedy.

"The superiority of the country aims-giver consists in two obvious advantages, not in the paucity of the means and opportunities afforded to the poor for the abuse of charity, —not in the fact of our rural districts being a sort of Arcadia, where innocence and gladness must necessarily be found, —for vice and temptation have no settled dwelling-place, they can wing their way across the freshest fields that ever were ploughed, —and the man who in London would be seen staggering from the gaudy portico of some gas-lighted palace of drunkenness, may equally booze away his time, wages, and intellect, at the door of the village tap. No; the advantages of the country alms-giver are, first, that he is brought into actual contact and communion with those he relieves; secondly, that the relief is rarely afforded in money; and as a natural consequence of both these positions, he is enabled to exercise a sort of controlling power over the employment of his own bounty. Wherever there are resident proprietors, nobility or gentry, this is done. The good and active wives of our under-paid clergy spare time from their busy families, and money from their narrow incomes, and bestow both on the poor, with a steady and considerate generosity, a degree of self-sacrifice, and a firm wisdom of purpose, which the narrow field into which all individual exertion must be compressed, may render more obscure, but not less meritorious. The wives and daughters of our aristocracy imitate their example. In vain would the flimsy and vapid works of the day, which pass for 'fashionable novels, ' defame that aristocracy as given up to frivolity and sin; and falsely representing all their women to be coquettes and all their men to be roués, stigmatise the whole class by generalising the vices of a few. Facts speak for themselves; and there will hardly be found a noble family in England whose daughters do not personally relieve and visit the poor in their immediate vicinity, and personally assist in the tuition and management of the village children. They are acquainted with the parents' names and employment—their abodes and their necessities; the relief given is consequently always serviceable—the object of that relief almost always grateful. They tacitly acknowledge as a serious and unavoidable duty a proper inquiry into the state of 'their own poor. '

"In that phrase may be found the watchword against evil alms-giving. The street-beggars of London are nobody's 'own poor. ' We have a dim and dismal consciousness that there are somewhere, we know not where, whole districts inhabited by 'low Irish, ' 'common vagrants, ' blind men, Italian boys, ragged and half-starved women and children; but who, in all the fashionable squares, streets, or terraces of the metropolis, considers any part of this mysterious population as their 'own poor? ' We know that they exist; for often in the day they flit across our path—dreary, idle, bat-like—and then disappear. How they live, what they do, we know not, neither do we inquire; sometimes we bestow a sixpence, sometimes not. If we have done so, what sacrifice have we made? How will the gift be used? Whom have we relieved? We have relieved the pain in our own hearts which God has mercifully willed the mere sight of suffering shall produce. As to the objects of our alms, they may be the better or they may be the worse for what we have done; they are not with us, they do not belong to us, they are gone back to the 'neighbourhood of St. Giles's, ' or some other place which we have heard is the resort of that class; they have homes somewhere, at least we suppose so, but it is no business ofours.

"Let me not be misunderstood: I do not undervalue the immense amount of real charity bestowed in London. Our crowded hospitals and asylums, our noble institutions for the relief of every species of distress, with their thousands and ten thousands of subscribers, would be a lesson against such opinions, if they existed, to say nothing of the private efforts made by benevolent individuals, each in his small and separate sphere: but I desire to address myself to the large body of 'thoughtless alms-givers, ' to convince them that the alternative is not whether they shall give rashly, or leave the street-beggar to the tender mercies of 'his own parish, '—whether, in brief, they shall give or not give; the alternative is, whether they shall give carelessly, and without inquiry, or whether they shall give considerately and on principle, as a Christain ought to give. I would fain persuade each man to consider the cases (they cannot be very numerous) which chance brings under his special and individual cognisance, as his 'own poor, ' to admit their conditional claims as though he were the resident landlord of an estate where they had homes, and to act upon the merits of each case, so that he may neither feel vague regret at not having relieved some chance beggar who he fears, after all, was 'a real object, ' nor be disappointed, as metropolitan alms-givers perpetually are, by the discovery of unworthiness and imposture.

"It is in vain to hope that any Utopian scheme of utility, or state enactment, will prevent the necessity of alms-giving. We have been told, on authority we may not question, that 'the poor shall never cease out of the land, ' and the only consideration left for us is, what should be our conduct to the poor.

"There can be no doubt that many indolent and worthless characters in the Metropolis subsist entirely on the daily renewed chance of hasty charity gleaned among the thousands who pass and repass them in the course of a few hours. But, on the other hand, there is no place where well-judged temporary assistance can be made of more real service, for there is no place where so much really temporary distress exists. The immense shifting population which the annual meeting of Parliament, (and the consequent gathering together of the principal families of Great Britain,) draws to the capital, creates of necessity a number of temporary employments: but these soon cease—the 'stagnant time of the year' follows 'the busy season; ' the nobility and gentry withdraw to their own estates, among their 'own poor; ' the regular tradesman counts his gains, and also, perhaps, departs on some cheerful holyday expedition after the toils of business; gay equipages and busy throngs cease to animate the half-deserted streets, and hundreds, who had been 'taken on' during the glut of occupation, are thrown out of work by the stopping of the vast machine of life which has been rapidly revolving for those few months. This is one class of the casual poor in London.

"Another class is composed of persons who have come to town to 'better themselves; ' who, relying on the certainty of wages and employment in this immense mart for labour, have travelled up with their families, and, after fruitless search for engagements in their several trades, become houseless wanderers in a city full of strangers, and have neither the means of supporting themselves where they are, nor of returning to the place from which they so rashly set out. This is a large and most pitiable class of 'street-beggars. ' Foot-sore, heart-weary, and vainly earnest, they trudge along, getting enough, perhaps, to shelter them at night and to fill the stomachs of their famishing children, but not enough, at any one time, to transport them back again; learning gradually to rely on this 'hand-to-mouth' system—this pernicious chance charity without inquiry, which ruins while it apparently relieves.

"I do not name the class of persons who have been reduced by great sickness, sudden losses, broken limbs, deprivation of relatives, &c. to ask alms, because these are not cases peculiar to the Metropolis; but these swell the number of street-beggars, haunting and waylaying us, with starved, dejected faces, and depending on 'the careless alms-giver' for a precarious subsistence.

"Now, it would be assuming a large average of charity to say that any one individual relieves two cases of distress per week, or 104 poor families in a year; but is it a large average of cases to be inquired into? It is true that personal inquiry is in many instances impossible; in many parts of London it is a service almost of danger to visit the poor, and a well-dressed person would be pelted and insulted in making the attempt. Many people who have a very generous sense of the claims of the distressed would be precluded from visiting them by the fact of their own time being entirely occupied; many, by the fear of carrying contagion from sick hovels to a young family; many, by their own bodily infirmities. But it does not follow that inquiry cannot be made. There are 'visitors' belonging to almost every charitable institution, whose express employment it is to make themselves personally acquainted with the truth of the representations on which alms are to be given. The Mendicity Society, for a small annual subscription, undertake the task of verifying every case sent to them by the subscriber, giving a written assurance of the circumstances being deserving or otherwise. Can any charity be more easily regulated than by this simple means?

"The second great advantage the country alms-giver has over the alms-giver in the streets of London consists in the fact, that his bounty is generally bestowed in kind, and not in money.

"Every young housekeeper knows, as the first great fact in domestic economy, the value of stores. The poor hare no stores. What they purchase, is purchased under all the combined disadvantages which waste, the necessity of present use, and the retail additions of prices, can impose. They starve, too, in attempting to procure minor quantities of the same articles of consumption as are in use in the classes above them, instead of substituting (as in other countries) plenty or sufficiency of a different kind. Tea, beer, and white bread, are things on which even the poorest will naturally proceed to lay out your alms: they cook what little meat they ever get in the most wasteful way: they have no habit, as in Scotland, of employing any cheap meal as an article of food. There is no greater evidence of the combined ignorance and improvidence of the lower classes, than the management of their diet. In the country, that ignorance and that improvidence are rendered less mischievous in their effects by a perpetual dependence in hours of sickness or distress, on 'the great house, ' 'the parsonage, ' &c., for assistance and advice; and, above all, for contributions from the 'store-room. ' In London, giving in kind, as it is called—giving coals, potatoes, meat, or orders for these things on one's own trades- people, is an incalculable benefit to the poor, who, from their retail method of purchasing, often pay three times as much as the rich do for the necessaries of life. The shilling given in the street, probably ill laid out, and at all events laid out under the disadvantages I have explained, is a poor substitute for the 'shilling's worth' of stores we might have given, had we 'taken thought for the poor. ' They take little thought for themselves, it is true; but before we indulge the feeling of irritation at their improvidence, let us strive to correct it: not always by reproof, for an empty stomach is an ill digester of rebukes; but by such practice as that I have referred to: and I will venture to state, that the amount of real relief will be quadrupled to the recipient at half the cost of casual alms to the donor.

"To affirm that it must be injurious to the poor to bestow on them what they have not earned, is to assert a paradox we should be loth to admit if applied to ourselves. How many of the comparatively rich have anxiously depended, in some hard hour of life, on a small loan; or craved a word of recommendation from a great man? Have they, at such times, invariably scanned their own deserts with a critical eye? Have they always balanced defect of prudence against necessity for aid? Would it not not seem strange to us, in moments like these, to be answered as we answer the poor? to be judged as we judge the poor? The self-dependence of the lower classes is a very dazzling theory, but it would borrow weight if we could point to the self-dependence of the upper classes as a practical example for imitation; and not reserve even begging (on a large scale) as an indulgence sacred to the rich. We are all dependent creatures: few men could honestly assert, whatever their position in life, that they never required or accepted aid, in any shape, from any human being. Why are the most helpless to be the class unassisted? Why is alms-giving from our superfluity (we rarely overdraw that fund) to be forbid, as folly? Charity requires regulating like all other human motives of action; and the great rule for metropolitan alms-giving should be, never, if possible, to give money, unless to redeem tools, defray a doctor's bill (that ruinous expense of the poor), make good an arrear of rent, or, in some discretionary cases, liquidate one of those small debts, the nonpayment of which frequently involve a whole family in irretrievable ruin. But these are matters in which the practical experience of every willing alms-giver may guide him; and to practical experience I leave it, anxious only to establish what appears to me the simplest and most obvious of all religious truths: namely, that we have no right to 'turn our face from any poor man; '

we have no right to refuse the alms we are especially commanded to bestow; and, therefore, it behoves us merely to attend to the manner of bestowing them. "